Criminals & Presidents

The Adventures of a Secret Service Agent

Tim Wood

authorHOUSE®

AuthorHouse™
1663 Liberty Drive
Bloomington, IN 47403
www.authorhouse.com
Phone: 1 (800) 839-8640

This book is a work of non-fiction. Unless otherwise noted, the author
and the publisher make no explicit guarantees as to the accuracy of
the information contained in this book and in some cases, names of
people and places have been altered to protect their privacy.

Published by AuthorHouse   03/04/2016

ISBN: 978-1-5049-8369-3 (sc)
ISBN: 978-1-5049-8367-9 (hc)
ISBN: 978-1-5049-8368-6 (e)

Library of Congress Control Number: 2016903681

Print information available on the last page.

This book is printed on acid-free paper.

For Maggie

Contents

Author's Note

If you've ever had the pleasure of sitting in a bar with a naval aviator and listening to the tales of flying a high-performance tactical jet aircraft, then you know, when he starts a story with the line "This is a true story. No shit," that you are about to be entertained.

During my tour of duty fighting crime in Las Vegas, Nevada, I had the pleasure of working with a small group of outstanding Secret Service agents. I was assigned to the Las Vegas Resident Agency from March 1, 1987, until June 16, 1991. During that time other agents assigned to the office transferred out and transferred in. The character "Donnie" is 75 percent Special Agent Ron Weiss and 25 percent Special Agent B. J. Flowers. Ron arrived at the Las Vegas Resident Agency shortly after my transfer in, and he was present during my entire tour of duty in the desert. My old buddy B.J. was in Las Vegas when I arrived and he left within a year, to be replaced by none other than the best friend any man could have—Special Agent Mike Fithen, aka the Beaver.

We went through three resident agents—the boss—during my tenure in Vegas; they kept getting promoted to higher grades, which meant a transfer, and they didn't seem to hang around too long. That's what happens when a supervisor has a good team working for him, he gets promoted. I was blessed with good supervisors, Chuck Brewster, Tom Spurlock, and the King of Fraud—Earl Devaney.

We worked with a group of outstanding assistant United States attorneys assigned to the United States Attorney's Office for the District of Nevada at Las Vegas. The character T.J. is a combination of L. J. O'Neale, Rick Pocker, Anne Perry, Russ Mayer, Camille Chamberlain, Paul Wommer, and Howard Zlotnick.

But without the Redhead, my wife of thirty-two years, none of this would have happened. She's the one who urged me to reapply with the Secret Service after my first application was rejected due to a hiring freeze.

This is a true story. No shit.

Chapter 1

The Snitch

When the bedside telephone rang in the middle of the night, I was usually pretty quick about waking up from a dead sleep and grabbing it before it rang a second time. After-hours phone calls were a way of life in the US Secret Service at the Las Vegas Resident Agency, and I think my reaction was plain old rote memory. Some nights, depending on what time it was and at which stage of sleep my feeble brain was in, I might miss the handle with my palm and just knock it off the cradle. But for the most part, I'd gotten real good at slapping it before that second ring.

And that's exactly what happened when the telephone rang at two that morning. My right arm made a big roundhouse swing from the middle of the bed over my chest and my hand slapped the receiver right out of the cradle. And I knocked the frickin' nightstand lamp on the floor with it.

Old Gus, our Labrador retriever, started barking and jumping up and down like he had just hit a royal flush, his mind no doubt on an early morning run or breakfast. Meanwhile, I was stumbling around next to the bed, in the dark of course—trying to find the telephone receiver, trying to keep one hand on Gus's collar and quiet him down, trying my best to make as little noise as possible, trying to be a good husband and *not* wake up the Redhead—when the nightstand lamp on her side of the bed came on.

I found the receiver and the Redhead grabbed Gus. They both disappeared down the hallway.

"Hello."

"Jesus Christ," said Donnie with a laugh. "Are you okay?"

My brain wasn't quite in full gear just yet; I still had that "sleep fog" going for me. I snapped out of it when I heard Donnie's voice.

"Yeah," I said. "What's up?"

"I hate to do this to you," he told me, "But the Beaver and I are at the Sahara working on an 'in custody' for cashing a stolen T-check with a counterfeit license, and Hilton Security just called with a counterfeit one hundred. They've got a suspect in custody. Can you run down to the Hilton and handle that for me?"

Donnie was a GS-13; he was the older guy in our meager staff of three agents. He'd already done a permanent protection detail, and this was his second tour in a field office working criminal investigations. That meant he was filling his "brag" sheet with a lot of "I did this" and "I did that" bullshit, looking for a promotion to GS-14. The Beaver and I were just GS-9s with only three years in the Secret Service. For Donnie, every case had the potential to be the big one, that whopping caper that would pull him over the top to a promotion. The Beaver and I just wanted to arrest bad guys.

"I checked the counterfeit when I was on the phone with the Hilton and it's that Colombian note," Donnie said, "We've been getting hit real hard with those." *No shit, the entire Secret Service was getting hammered with that Colombian counterfeit hundred-dollar bill.*

"Yep," I said, "I'm on my way."

That was Las Vegas in the 1980s; three Secret Service agents working their butts off in that 24/7 gambling oasis in the desert. I pulled on my Las Vegas uniform—blue jeans, cowboy boots, and an untucked Hawaiian shirt to conceal my Smith and Wesson Model 19 and handcuffs.

The Redhead was back in bed when I walked out of the bathroom. I kissed her goodbye and told her I'd see her when I see her. Gus followed me to the garage door; I rubbed his head and said, "Go back to bed, buddy; it's too early for breakfast." I jumped in my G-ride, a beautiful white IROC-Z Chevy Camaro, and drove to the Las Vegas Hilton.

The Hilton security officers had a fifty-one-year-old female tourist from Denver sitting in their suspect interview room. Her husband was sitting in the security office lobby when I walked in. I took a good look at him as I walked by; he looked like your typical run-of-the-mill retired postal worker. Jean was very cooperative with me and I got the feeling right away that she wasn't a counterfeiter.

She gave me permission to search her purse and I found close to a thousand dollars in hundred-dollar bills. I examined each one and they were all genuine Federal Reserve notes (FRNs) printed by the US Treasury. I asked her if she had any idea where she got the counterfeit note. "No," she told me, "Ernie went to the bank this morning before we left and got five one-hundred-dollar bills in cash for our trip." The chances of a bank giving out a counterfeit note to a customer were slim; not beyond happening, but it would be a very rare exception if a bank didn't catch it as counterfeit.

I asked her where she'd been gambling that day. "We were here at the Hilton, we went by the Sands for a while, the Holiday, the Stardust and Sully's, then back here." She smiled real big and continued, "I hit an eleven-hundred-dollar jackpot at Sully's right after dinner!"

Sully's. Frickin' Sully's!

There were two or three casinos in Las Vegas that never sent our office counterfeit notes, or at least their banks never sent us the counterfeit notes. Sully's was one of those. We had surmised for a long time that Sully's was just passing any counterfeit notes they took back to the public; we had no proof of that, and there wasn't much we could do or wanted to do about it. It was just odd that we never got any counterfeit from Sully's.

I walked out to the lobby of the security office and, after identifying myself to Mr. Ernie; I asked if I could examine the cash in his wallet. Ernie had six one-dollar bills and a five-dollar bill. "That's all the cash you have?" I asked him.

"Hey," he said, "you must not be married." I liked his sense of humor. Then he said to me, "What's gonna happen to Jean?"

"That all depends," I said, "but first, I have to make sure she's not the reincarnated Bonnie Parker." I didn't think he got my wisecrack because he gave me a quizzical frown. "Have a seat and relax," I said. "I just need to check a couple of more things. Do you have any objection to me searching your hotel room?"

"No, no! None at all! Whatever you need," he replied. "We want to cooperate with you. I know you're just doing your job."

Jean and Ernie were staying at the Hilton, and she gave me written consent to search their room. A casino security officer went up with me and I did a thorough search of their belongings and didn't find any incriminating evidence. Nothing to indicate she or Ernie were in the counterfeiting business. However, from the looks of the contents of Jean's suitcase, ol' Ernie was in for a wild time in room 1487! I hoped the old guy was up for it.

Back at the security office I seized the Colombian counterfeit hundred-dollar bill and wrote Jean a Secret Service "receipt for contraband."

"How do I get my one hundred dollars back?" she asked me. That was probably the number one question most innocent passers asked. "You don't," I told her. "That's why it's against the law. It's worthless; Uncle Sam didn't print it. The last person holding a counterfeit note is out of luck." Jean cocked her head and began to protest, but stopped short and I could see in her eyes she was beginning to realize she was a victim.

I walked out to my Camaro and glanced at my watch. It was close to five-fifteen in the morning. I fired up the IROC-Z and turned the air conditioner on full blast. I picked up my Motorola handset for the radio and called to see if Donnie or the Beaver were in their cars. "Hey, anybody out there?"

The Beaver answered up, "Did you do any good?"

"Naw, innocent pass. You need some help?"

"I'm with Donnie; whattaya think?" Obviously Donnie was not on the air and the Beaver loved to bust Donnie's balls. "Meet us at Binion's for breakfast and we'll fill you in. Donnie's buying."

The Beaver was a big guy, a little over six foot and about two-eighty. He had a massive chest and arms. He was a power lifter and could easily squat six hundred pounds. He got his nickname when he started on the job in the Los Angeles Field Office (LAFO). He had brownish-red hair, a hint of freckles, and those cute dimples when he smiled. He was the spitting image of Theodore Cleaver. In the face, anyway.

I remember one Monday morning, I walked into to his office with a cup of coffee and asked about his weekend. "Good," he said. "I went to Reno for the powerlifting championships. I won my age class, benched four-fifty." *Benched 450 pounds! Are you kidding me?* We worked out at the gym every day, and I didn't realize he was training for a competition. "I wasn't," he said. "I just entered on a whim. I was just looking to get out of Vegas for the weekend with my angel. So we drove up to Reno."

I met Donnie and the Beaver at the main restaurant in Binion's Horseshoe Hotel and Casino downtown on Fremont Street. Donnie was wound up (which wasn't unusual) and he ordered his normal healthy breakfast of granola and yogurt. The Beaver and I had T-bone steak and eggs…with home fries and toast, for a buck and change. That was one of the great things about Vegas in the eighties, really good cheap eats.

Donnie said he and the Beaver "rolled" the suspect, she had agreed to work for us and introduce an undercover agent to the suspects. "No shit," I said. "We haven't had a good caper like that it a while. So what happened?"

The girl's name was Tammy. She was twenty-three years old with bleached blonde hair and Donnie said she could use some braces. Tammy claimed she was just hanging out at the downtown casinos killing time playing video poker machines, although they didn't believe that for one minute; based on her attire, chances were good she was a prostitute.

She said around eight the previous night a guy named Roland had approached her at the bar at the Horseshoe Casino. Tammy said she'd met Roland about three or four months ago and she had cashed a check for him. Roland paid her fifty dollars for cashing the check and she claimed that was the only time she'd seen Roland. Tonight Roland again offered her fifty dollars to cash a check for him and she said, "What the heck; I could use an extra fifty bucks."

Donnie said he asked Tammy if the first check she cashed for Roland was a Treasury check and she innocently asked, "What's a Treasury check?"

The Beaver looked at me and said, "She's not the sharpest crayon in the box."

Tammy insisted she didn't know anything else about Roland. She said she didn't have a telephone number for him and she didn't know his last name or where he lived. She thought he was a heroin addict, though, because he wore long-sleeved shirts and he was super fidgety.

Tammy said Roland took her to a photo booth in the Horseshoe and had her take four photos of herself. She said the first time she cashed a check for him, Roland had approached her at the El Cortez Casino bar and he did the same thing. Tonight, she said he took the photos and told her to meet him at the main bar at the Fremont Casino at midnight. Tammy said she went to the Fremont and waited, but by twelve thirty Roland hadn't shown up. She started to leave and as she navigated her way out through the casino, she ran smack-dab into him when he came out of the men's room. Roland was with another guy named Paul. She'd never seen Paul before. They took her out to the parking garage and when they got in the garage stairwell, Paul handed her an envelope containing the check and the counterfeit driver's license. Roland told her to meet him at the main casino bar in the Four Queens at two o'clock in the afternoon and to bring all $365 from the proceeds of the check.

Tammy said Roland was a tall guy, maybe six foot two, about thirty with blondish hair and really bad skin. She said Paul was forty-five or so, short, just a bit taller than her, slicked-back black hair, and he was skinny as a rail.

They didn't tell her where to cash the check and she didn't think they'd followed her to the Sahara. This was important, because if Roland and Paul had seen her get pinched by casino security, all bets were off. If they knew she was arrested for cashing the check and didn't go to jail, Roland and Paul wouldn't get with in fifty feet of her again, and we wouldn't be able to use her as an informant.

Donnie said they leaned on her pretty hard to make sure she was telling the truth. They gave it the old good cop, bad cop routine, with Donnie being her friend and the Beaver pretending she was lying. "She's full of shit," said Beaver to Donnie, right in front of her. "We're wasting our time on this. Let's just book her and go home." Donnie patiently explained the perjury law to her, Title 18 United States Code Section 1001. It is a felony to lie to a federal agent. The Beaver took a bite of T-bone steak and chuckled, "I told her it was a big-time felony to lie to me."

Once they decided she was being up front with them about the events leading to her arrest that night, they got in touch with the Sahara Casino security guys and reviewed the video from the casino surveillance cameras. Donnie said they could see Tammy walking around the Sahara Casino and up to the cashier's cage to cash the check. They didn't see anyone walking with her or near her, or anyone near the cage that appeared to be watching her.

Donnie told me they cut her loose at about five o'clock that morning and he gave her specific instructions to be at our office at noon and, most important, to talk to no one. *Keep your mouth shut. Tight. Do not tell a soul that your little check-cashing scam went haywire and the cops interviewed you.*

That sounds pretty simple, but you'd be surprised how many informants just can't keep their mouths shut. Donnie had an informant one time that almost got killed because he could not resist telling his dope fiend friends he was working with the Secret Service on a *big* case.

As an investigator you just never know if a suspect is telling the truth; you can only go on your experience and your gut feeling when you interview someone and turn him or her into an informant. If we were in L.A., we would have immediately polygraphed her; but in Las Vegas, the nearest Secret Service polygraph examiner was actually in Los Angeles, and we didn't have the time to wait. We had to move. When you're trying to work a case back to the source, a good informant is invaluable and time is of the essence.

After breakfast, Donnie went to the Horseshoe Casino Security Office and then stopped by the Fremont to see if the surveillance cameras picked up any shots of Roland or Paul meeting with Tammy. From there, he was going over to the US Attorney's office to meet with T.J, the duty AUSA (Assistant United States Attorney). to discuss our plan to introduce an undercover agent to the suspects.

The Beaver went by the Las Vegas Metropolitan Police Department (LVMPD) Bunco/Forgery Squad to see if they had anything on these guys. I drove over to our office to inventory the Colombian counterfeit one hundred and write up a short report on the interview of Jean.

Donnie had put together a solid, but simple plan to arrest Paul and Roland. And it followed the book; all good plans follow the book, and you have to keep it simple; because Murphy's Law applies—"if it can go wrong, it will go wrong." We were going to wire up Tammy and have her meet with Roland around two that afternoon at the Four Queens Casino bar, as Roland had instructed her. We would have her engage Roland in some good incriminating conversation. including Paul's participation and give him the proceeds from the stolen US Treasury check.

Donnie wanted her to ask Roland if she could do some more work for him and if Roland agreed, we would have her get another stolen Treasury check and another counterfeit driver's license from them and do it again. Donnie told her it was very important to get his last name, where he lived and a telephone number from him. Our plan was to then have Tammy introduce her boyfriend (me) to Roland and Paul and get them to include me on a deal. If they didn't bite on her offer, case over; but we would have some solid incriminating evidence in Roland's own voice admitting his participation in the crime.

When Donnie got back to our office he told me he reviewed the surveillance camera tapes at the Horseshoe and the Fremont. He said he could see the backs of the heads of Tammy and some guy with light-colored hair sitting at the bar at the Horseshoe, but that was about it. No good frontal shots. The cameras at the Fremont Casino were even worse; Donnie found footage of Tammy sitting at the bar and at around twelve thirty and getting up and walking away. No footage of a tall blond male and a short, skinny black-haired male. The Beaver said Bunco/Forgery had nothing on a Roland or a Paul.

Tammy showed up at our office on time and that was a good start. Informants come in all shapes and sizes, as you can imagine, and most of them need repeated verbal instructions, and a tight leash. The absolute worst informant was the reformed crook that thought he was now on the right side of this godly profession... with a license to take the investigation wherever he wanted to take the investigation. The absolute best informant was a pissed off-girlfriend, with some sense. Tammy was just your average I-don't-wanna-go-to jail-I'll-help-you-any-way-I-can informant.

Donnie and I reinterviewed Tammy to make sure there were no holes in her story. Donnie really tore into her; gone was Mister Nice Guy. "Just remember," he scolded her, "if you are lying to us about this I will make sure the US Attorney charges you with everything under the sun. You'll wish you had never met me."

Shit, now he had her bawling. "I swear," she exclaimed. "That's what happened, I swear it is!"

Donnie ran through the plan with her at least a half dozen times. This would be our only shot to get into these two crooks. We still weren't sure if they were part of a stolen Treasury check gang or a counterfeit identification gang or both or something totally different. The Secret Service had jurisdiction over stolen and forged US Treasury checks and counterfeit identification documents, so both parts of her cashing a stolen Treasury check with a counterfeit identification were in our bailiwick. Most forgery rings will cash any type of stolen check they can get their hands on. But that's the kind of information an undercover agent can discover once he gets in with the ring.

The fact (if it were true) that Roland had approached Tammy and she had cashed a stolen check for him once before made us think these guys were running a forgery ring. Bad guys typically recruit "runners" to cash the stolen checks so they can insulate themselves. But you just never know until you start investigating. One thing was for sure, if I could get into this gang as an undercover agent, this could turn into a big case.

Tammy was supposed to meet Roland at the main bar in the Four Queens at two o'clock that afternoon; we bought her a sandwich and got her all wired up. At about one o'clock, Donnie and the Beaver drove her to the Union Plaza and I met up with Gaming Enforcement Agent Vinnie G. from the Nevada Gaming Control Board.

Vinnie was a wizard in a casino camera surveillance room, and he was more than willing to help us with surveillance in a casino. Bad guys always seemed to want to have a meeting in a casino, which I could never quite figure out because almost every inch of a casino is covered by cameras.

* * *

The three of us loved working with gaming agents. In Nevada gaming is a privilege, not a right, so when the Gaming Control Board agents showed up at a casino, they didn't *ask*, they *told* the casino people to clear the camera surveillance room. It was a wonderful and powerful investigative tool. I had worked with Vinnie on many occasions, my favorite being a case he had caught at the Aladdin Hotel and Casino involving counterfeit passports.

The Aladdin was giving away five hundred dollars in free chips to new customers. All they had to do was show identification at the casino cage and voilà, a free gambling stake! Casino security had identified a group of Chinese gentleman who seemed to be repeat customers...same faces, but different names on their passports. Vinnie G. gave me a call one day and asked if I would be interested in helping them out. *Heck, yeah!*

On a Saturday night I met with Vinnie and three other gaming agents at the Aladdin and he took over the casino surveillance room to watch and tape the suspects fraudulently obtaining the free chips. Vinnie and I walked through the casino to a nondescript door, up some stairs to another nondescript door. Vinnie knocked...I was half expecting him to utter a password. Some big guy cracked the door open. Badges flashed and Vinnie said, very calmly, "Nevada Gaming Control Board enforcement agent." He nodded toward me and said to the big guy, "You don't need to know who this is. You'll have to vacate the camera surveillance room...we need to use it."

"Yes sir." came the reply. No hesitation. No buts. About a dozen guys got up from their desks and walked out. Vinnie locked the door behind them. Then he began working the surveillance cameras. When one of the other gaming agents saw three Chinese men walk up to the casino cage, he alerted us on Vinnie's handheld radio. Vinnie operated those cameras like a pro; he followed the targets as they stood at the cage, presented the passports to the cashier, were given the free chips, and walked to a blackjack table, recording everything. The other gaming agents, who were watching the suspects from the casino floor, confirmed with the Aladdin security manager that these were the same men who had previously used different names and passports to receive five hundred dollars in free chips.

Once the targets started gambling, Vinnie got on his handheld radio and called for the arrest. We walked out of the surveillance room and down the stairs. We met up with the three other gaming agents and walked through the casino toward the blackjack table where the Chinese crooks were playing. As we walked five abreast down the center aisle of the Aladdin, patrons parted; they stopped gambling, they stopped talking, and some probably stopped breathing. It was a scene straight out of *Gunsmoke*, just like Marshal Dillon and Chester walking into the Long Branch Saloon to deal with some card cheats.

It turned out the passports were Chinese and I had no way to determine their authenticity. They had to be counterfeit, but the AUSA declined to federally prosecute them. Just as well, the Las Vegas local courts dealt harshly with card cheats—don't ever try to cheat a casino. The Nevada State Prison was full of people who'd been caught cheating.

* * *

Once Donnie and Tammy got to the Union Plaza, Beaver went into the Four Queens and found a seat down at the corner end of the bar, where he had a good view of the scene. Donnie had Tammy walk from the Union Plaza down Fremont Street into the Four Queens. Donnie kept his distance and followed her in. Meanwhile, I met Vinnie G. at the Four Queens hotel registration desk and he took me up to the casino surveillance room.

A few minutes after two o'clock Roland walked into the Four Queens and sat next to Tammy at the bar. I had the receiver for the transmitter Tammy was wearing, but the connection was shitty; I could pick up some of the conversation, but it kept fading in and out. I just hoped the tape recorder in her purse was working. Tammy slipped Roland an envelope with $365 that Donnie had given her. He counted the cash, slipped her fifty bucks, and then put his arm around her shoulders and whispered something to her. I couldn't make out with he said, but I did hear her reply, as she removed his arm from her shoulder, "Not today, honey." That I heard…loud and clear. My gut tightened up, because now Tammy was off script; whatever she said next could make or break this caper.

She came through with flying colors when, without missing a beat, she asked Roland if she could have his telephone number. Vinnie and I saw him reach for a cocktail napkin and start scribbling on it with a Keno pencil. Then, I heard her say she'd like to do some more work for him, that the driver's license was perfect! The UHF transmitter was intermittent again and all I heard him reply was "Paul…best."

Roland got up from his bar stool and gave her a peck on the cheek and walked away.

Vinnie worked the surveillance cameras and we were able to visually follow him out of the main casino exit onto Fremont Street. Beaver was working his way around the casino to keep an eye on Roland's destination, while Vinnie and I scooted out to the parking garage where we jumped into my Camaro, standing by for Beaver to provide a direction of travel. As per the plan, Tammy got off the bar stool five minutes later and started walking toward the Union Plaza to meet Donnie. You have to love an informant that actually follows direction.

The Beaver radioed me that Roland got on a city bus at the intersection of Fremont and Las Vegas Boulevard and was heading south toward the Strip. That was too easy to follow; so far, things were working out pretty smoothly with this meet. Vinnie and I followed the bus south on Las Vegas Boulevard. At a bus stop near the Stardust Hotel and Casino, we saw Roland get off and walk toward the casino entrance. Vinnie got some great pictures of Roland with his telephoto lens camera as he stepped off the bus and casually looked to his right…right at us.

Donnie got on the radio and told us to discontinue the surveillance, no sense taking the chance of burning ourselves. He said Tammy got some great conversation with Roland, his telephone number, and he wanted her to call him for more work.

A moving surveillance is hard to do with only two or three cars and that was a problem we always faced at the Las Vegas Resident Agency. Sure, we had the support of the mother ship back in at the Los Angeles Field Office, and the big boss in L.A. would always send guys to help us out with undercover meets, if we gave them enough notice. But we didn't always have a lot of notice to put these deals together. Consequently, we worked very closely with our sister Treasury agency ATF (Alcohol, Tobacco, and Firearms) and occasionally the boys at DEA (Drug Enforcement Agency). If a casino was remotely involved in the scenario, the Gaming Enforcement guys would be involved. We tended to stay away from asking Freddie, Bernie, and Irving (FBI) for assistance... not because we didn't appreciate their help, but the "Feebies" tend to want to control everything and Secret Service agents like being in charge. It's in our DNA...it's our nature. Individual Secret Service agents are given a tremendous responsibility with our Protective Mission. Thus, we are type-A...maybe even type-A plus. So we avoided routinely working with the FBI.

We all met Donnie back at the office and he and Beaver debriefed Tammy. I listened to the tape recording and I could clearly hear Roland and Tammy's conversation. We now had him on tape admitting he gave Tammy the check and the counterfeit driver's license. And he handed up Paul as the maker of the counterfeit identification...it was perfect.

Unfortunately, like most undercover deals, this one would take time to develop. We used to call it working on "bad guy time": crooks are undependable, especially when they are drug addicts, and they don't work the "day shift."

Over the next week Donnie had Tammy place some consensually recorded and monitored telephone calls to Roland. He either didn't answer, was high on heroin, or was too busy to talk to Tammy…we were getting frustrated with the slow pace of this case and I was starting to think Roland thought she'd been pinched that night at the Sahara and he was keeping his distance, afraid she was snitching for the cops (which she was). We discussed the possibility that she was scamming us—meaning she'd contacted Roland on her own and "ratted" us out to him. The old double cross. We decided to polygraph her; Donnie got one of the polygraph examiners from the LAFO to come over to Vegas.

The polygraph is an excellent investigative tool. Bad guys and defense attorneys are always saying, "The results of a polygraph are not admissible in court." *Yeah? Well, big deal.* The whole point of a polygraph is to help an investigator determine if a suspect is lying to him. The actual instrument just advises the examiner that on some particular question, the suspect has had a different physiological reaction, which indicates to the investigator that the suspect *may* be untruthful. The post-test interrogation is where you get the truth out of them.

I was never a polygraph examiner, but we utilized polygraphs all the time and I used to watch the post-test interview through the one-way mirrors in the polygraph suite. The investigator, or rather the examiner, is the one who gets the truth out of the suspect, and Secret Service polygraph examiners are the best interrogators in the business.

Luckily, Tammy passed with flying colors; the agent from L.A. who conducted the examination said she had no issues on the two key questions we wanted her to answer. At least now we knew she wasn't double-crossing us, and she had told the truth about that night at the Sahara. Now, we just needed Roland to take her telephone call and get this caper moving.

Donnie thought about ending it and just getting an arrest warrant for Roland—we had probable cause for an arrest. But with Tammy passing the polygraph we wanted to keep trying to get ahold of Roland and get some good confirming evidence on Paul and arrest him. T.J. wanted us to keep trying for now, to see if we could get an undercover agent to buy a counterfeit driver's license from Roland and Paul, and work Tammy out of the picture. That's the book on these capers; you have to try and protect the informant as much as possible, for as long as possible. Eventually, if there is a trial, the informant is going to have to testify, and we told them that up front…but in the meantime, you have give them some cover.

At the Las Vegas Resident Agency, time, or the lack of time, was always a problem. With only three working agents in that 1980s crime-ridden city, something else was always coming up.

Chapter 2

Getting to Las Vegas

It was fall, and the oaks and hickories of central Missouri were in full color. I was sitting on the grass across from the Ellis Library at the University of Missouri; the Memorial Student Union was on my left. Jessie Hall and the Columns were down Lowry Street to my right. It was a normal class day and students were walking from one side of campus to the other. I was actually getting close to graduating from college.

As I sat in the shade on that day, I pondered my future. Reality was starting to set in. I didn't *really* have a plan and I was starting to realize that I really needed a plan. The idea of just getting a "job" when I graduated sounded so mundane. I had started college majoring in forestry, but this was the 1970s. Jimmy Carter was President, the economy was dog shit, and most of the guys graduating with a degree in forestry were not working in the forestry business; jobs in that industry were few and far between. So after five semesters, I'd changed my major to education. Although I had no real burning desire to be a teacher, after some research, I'd figured it was the quickest way to use all the college science classes I'd taken as a forestry major and get my degree. All I needed were the education degree requirements.

I had just walked through the Memorial Union and saw a United States Marine Corps recruiting booth set up with a couple of marines in their blue pants with the red stripe and tan shirt. I remember looking at those two marines, a captain and a lieutenant, and thinking they were two impressive-looking men. So, as I sat there on that Indian summer afternoon, contemplating my future, it suddenly hit me, *you only live once.* I would become a United States marine.

I had always thought about the Marine Corps—in fact, I had almost enlisted after I quit school the semester I'd become disillusioned with forestry as a career. That day, I got up and walked back into the Memorial Union and started a thirty-minute conversation with the captain about my future. And it was absolutely the best decision I have ever made...and that includes asking the Redhead to marry me, because had I *not* made the decision to join the United States Marine Corps, I would have *never* met that gal, plain and simple.

A few weeks later I was sitting in the recruiter's Kansas City office, completing the paperwork to sign up for the Officer Candidate Program. The Marine Corps must have been short of pilots that fall, because the captain was really pushing the Naval Aviation Program to the handful of wide-eyed college students that morning. *That sounds like fun. Where do I sign?* A pilot had to have perfect twenty-twenty vision, and mine was just a little off, but the recruiter said I could become a naval flight officer as a radar intercept officer in the F4 Phantom or a bombardier/

navigator in the A6 Intruder. I passed the aviation written test and I signed on the dotted line.

I went to Officer Candidate School the next summer and was commissioned a second lieutenant after I graduated from the University of Missouri in December 1977. The next month I started my Marine Corps career at the Basic School in Quantico, Virginia, a six-month training course for all newly commissioned officers.

The Naval Flight Training Command in Pensacola, Florida, was next. And those wings of gold were pinned on my chest in the spring of '79. I reported to the A6 Replacement Air Group at Marine Corps Air Station (MCAS) Cherry Point, North Carolina, a month later. After twelve months I was a fully trained bombardier/navigator and ready for the fleet. I had two choices of duty stations: The 2nd Marine Air Wing in Cherry Point or the 3rd Marine Air Wing in El Toro, California. That was a no-brainer. California...Southern California was the place for me. I loaded my brand-new pickup truck with all my worldly possessions and drove west.

I made a surprise stop at the Diamond's restaurant in Gray Summit, Missouri, to say hello to my dad before popping in on my mom at home. My dad was the manager of this truck stop–type restaurant. The Diamond's was a local landmark; it had been in business since the 1920s. It started out as the Banana Stand, at the intersection of Route 66 and Highway 100 in Villa Ridge, Missouri, selling sandwiches, along with the local produce, to hungry travelers. Business was so good the owner eventually built a permanent building to house his restaurant. My dad started working there when he was in high school, and would be the manager for over fifty years.

The original building burned to the ground late one night in 1948. My mom used to tell the story of that night. When Dad got word the building was on fire and he and Mom headed out from their home in Washington, Missouri, flying down Highway 100 the twelve miles or so to Route 66. By the time they got there, the place was a total loss, but Mom saved a coffee can full of melted pennies; and that's all that was left.

The owner rebuilt the restaurant, and added a motel and employee bunkhouse. Some of the guys Dad hired lived in the bunkhouse. Dad grew up during the Depression and served in World War II, and to my dad these "down on their luck" veterans just needed a job and a place to sleep. Most of them had a drinking problem, and every now and then, one of them wouldn't show up for work and Dad would say, "He's on a drunk." But when the guy sobered up, his job was always waiting for him. Dad was like that... he had a big heart.

He always said, "Nobody leaves the Diamond's hungry." And what he meant by that was if a hobo came in and asked him for a job to earn something to eat, Dad would gladly give them a free meal; but if a patron walked out without paying, he'd call the Sheriff's Office in a heartbeat. Dad used to always tell me, "If they would have just told me they were broke before they ordered food, I would have gladly bought them lunch."

I started working at the Diamond's when I was twelve years old, cleaning tables, washing dishes, and sweeping out the basement. I worked there every summer up to and including my college days. Busboy, dishwasher, short order cook, but my favorite job was working outside at the filling station. My brother, sisters, and all my cousins worked there in the summers, too; all the kids in the family always had a guaranteed summer job working for my dad.

I continued on my first coast-to-coast road trip and eventually made it to California. As I drove south on Interstate 5 toward MCAS El Toro, I remember gripping the steering wheel of my pickup like I was hanging off a thousand-foot cliff and letting go would plunge me to my death. I'd never seen such crazy bumper-to-bumper traffic flowing at seventy-five miles per hour! Obviously, the speed limit didn't mean shit around there. And then I smelled it, the orange groves of Orange County, California. What a beautiful smell. To this day a whiff of orange essence will take me back to El Toro.

The 3rd Marine Air Wing assigned me to the Bats of VMA (AW) 242, one of the finest Marine All-Weather Attack A6E squadrons in the Fleet Marine Force. Two thousand accident-free flight hours later (with a few close calls) it was time to move on. I put in an application as a special agent with the United States Secret Service.

After a very long, drawn-out application and interview process, I was offered a position as a special agent and reported to the LAFO on the first Monday after Thanksgiving in 1984. Before my career was over, the Secret Service would move the Redhead and me six times: Los Angeles to Las Vegas, Las Vegas to DC, DC to Seattle, Seattle to Boise, Boise to DC, DC back to Seattle. I would arrest over a hundred criminals and protect presidents, vice presidents, former presidents and numerous foreign heads of state.

I started my career in the LAFO Forgery Squad, where 99 percent of all new agents were assigned. The LAFO was a large field office with almost one hundred agents. The Forgery Squad investigated stolen or forged US Treasury checks. In the eighties, paper government checks were still the primary way Uncle Sam paid his bills. EFT (electronic funds transfer) was just getting started. I even got a paper paycheck every two weeks in those days. Los Angeles is a big city and we had plenty of forged check cases to work.

One Monday morning, after I'd just returned to the field office from the training academy, the SAIC (special agent in charge) called an all-hands office meeting. I walked into our big conference room a little early and grabbed a seat in the back row against the wall. There were about five us already in the room and we were bullshitting about nothing in particular, when one of the admin ladies walked in with a new guy. And this new guy wasn't shy; he walked around the small group of early arrivals and shook hands with everybody introducing himself. The room began to rapidly fill up and the next thing I know, the new guy sits down next to me. The first thing I noticed about this guy is his size. *This guy's looks like he could give the wall a forearm and break right through it.* We struck up a conversation. He said he was former policeman from Salt Lake City. The Beaver had just entered my life.

The LAFO had satellite offices, called Resident Agencies (RAs), in Santa Ana, Santa Barbara, Riverside, and Las Vegas. Our geographical area of jurisdiction was L.A. County, Orange County, Santa Barbara County, Riverside and San Bernardino County, and damn near all of Nevada. The RAs were very thinly staffed...a resident agent and two or three special agents

The LAFO had the Forgery Squad, the Counterfeit Squad, the Fraud Squad, the Special Investigations Squad, the Protective Intelligence Squad, and the Protection Squad. I was hoping my next assignment would be the Counterfeit Squad. One of the reasons I was attracted to the Secret Service was counterfeit money. US currency had always intrigued me. If you look at an FRN, it's a thing of beauty. The detail in the engraving is a work of art. The intaglio printing gives the bill that rough, three-dimensional look and feel. And to think a skilled craftsman...albeit a criminal, but still skilled in his craft, could reproduce those notes was very interesting. And I wanted to catch those guys.

I knew that L.A. was just the first step of my career. Most agents spend their first few years honing their investigative skills in a field office before being assigned to a permanent protective detail—the President, Vice President, or one of the former presidents' details. I had one goal for my future—PPD, the Presidential Protective Division. The A team, that's what I had my eye on. I would settle for nothing less.

* * *

In the mid-eighties, Reagan was president and, of course, he and Mrs. Reagan spent a lot of time in Los Angeles and Santa Barbara. Their children also lived in the L.A. area and the Secret Service assigned agents to protect them. Former president Ford lived in Palm Springs, out in the Riverside RA's area of operation. Every agent in L.A. seemed to always be busy with some type of protection assignment. Standing post for President Reagan or the First Lady, doing advances for former president Ford, or being assigned to one of numerous foreign heads of state that visited Los Angeles.

One of my first PPD post-standing assignments was at the Century Plaza Hotel in Century City. I was assigned to the President's holding room. My instructions were simple: No unauthorized people were allowed into the holding room. I was pretty pumped about that assignment. I was just a GS-7 in those days, fresh out of training, and I figured for sure they'd stick me in a stairwell, but the holding room for the President of the United States? That was a choice assignment.

At the appointed time, I heard on my radio that President Reagan was moving to the holding room. I was concentrating on making sure I was doing my job, effectively and efficiently. Because when the President showed up, so would the agents from PPD and I wanted them to take notice of me. Rumor among the young guys was, you don't call PPD—PPD calls you. So impressing the bosses and other agents assigned to the President was key in advancing to that detail.

President Reagan walked into the holding room from a door at one end of that large conference room with an entourage that was unexpected, to say the least. I guess I was expecting to see the President and a handful of PPD agents. What I got was a gaggle of very important-looking people. Holy shit, everybody had an earpiece for a radio, everybody had an official lapel pin, *who is who?* I was overwhelmed. *Now what do I do?* I had been instructed that when President Reagan entered the room, I would be "pushed off" to take up a post in the hallway outside the door. The PPD shift, working the inner perimeter, would handle security in the room once the President entered. *Okay, he's here. Which one of these guys is going to "push" me off?*

I didn't panic; I was just concerned I would fuck this up. It turned out there was no need to worry. President Reagan and his entourage kept walking and walking fast, through the room to the opposite door. They didn't stop; they didn't even slow down, for Pete's sake. President Reagan walked past me, looked right at me, and gave me a nod. President Ronald Reagan just gave me a nod!

Securing a venue for the President of the United States is a major undertaking. Preparations start days before the visit and require many hours and extensive manpower the day of the visit. It is a process; a very thorough, detailed process. I'd been standing in that holding room for hours. And in my young, just-out-of-training mind I had spent hours worrying about something I didn't need to worry about. As I watched the door close behind President Reagan, it hit me. *I am a United States Secret Service agent; those PPD agents walking with the President are the same as me. The only reason they are with the President is because they have more experience and time on the job.*

Months later, I was assigned to suite security at the Beverly Hilton Hotel for First Lady Nancy Reagan while she was in Los Angeles for a few days visiting her family and some old Hollywood friends. The agents assigned to her protective detail went with her whenever she left the hotel, but they left me and another LAFO agent to man the Secret Service security room and keep the suite secure during her absence.

I was told Mrs. Reagan liked to cook when she was in L.A. and away from the White House. One morning when reporting for duty in the Secret Service Security Room at the hotel, one of the

PPD agents told me she was in the suite baking. It looked like she would be in the suite most of the morning, so the shift leader told me to rotate in with his PPD agents securing the hallway and suite door. The shift leader was Tim McCarthy, the agent shot by John Hinckley when Hinckley fired off five shots at President Reagan back in 1981 at the Washington, DC, Hilton Hotel. I was very excited to be assigned to work with a real Secret Service hero, a man who took a bullet for the President.

Later that morning, it was my turn to hold the security post on Mrs. Reagan's suite door. After a few minutes, the suite door opened behind me, and there stood Nancy Reagan holding a plate full of freshly baked cookies. I think she was a little surprised to see me. She didn't know me, as I was not permanently assigned to her detail, and so she kind of paused, and looked at my lapel pin, which identified me as an agent.

"Good morning, Mrs. Reagan. Can I help you with something?" I said.

She handed me the plate of cookies and said, "Here, these are for you and the boys."

It didn't take us long to devour those cookies. When I got home late that evening and told the Redhead that story she was incredulous, "What? You didn't save any of those cookies? You guys ate Nancy Reagan's cookies?"

"Well yeah we ate the cookies," I said. "What was I supposed to do with them? Frame them for the mantel?"

* * *

I'd been keeping an eye on what was happening in the Las Vegas RA, as arrest reports always seemed to be flowing out of that office. Rumor was the guys in Vegas were quite busy and they all seemed to have a good reputation, not only within the LAFO, but service-wide. When they left Vegas, they were going to their first choice of assignment.

As young agents at the LAFO, we always had the Western Protective Detail hanging over our heads. That detail was charged with protecting President Reagan's children, an important assignment, no doubt, because all of the protective missions were very important, but that's not what I wanted to do.

I had to position myself to get assigned to PPD. It seemed to me that assignments to the Western Protective Detail just came up randomly and young agents ready for their first protection assignment would be plucked from the ranks on a Friday and told to report on Monday. *No thanks; I have to get to Washington, DC.* The Las Vegas RA was starting to look like a really good way to get there. First, it would get me out of my twice-daily two-hour commute from Orange County to the LAFO. Secondly, the Redhead and I could actually afford to buy a house in the Vegas real estate market, something that was not happening in Southern California in the eighties for a GS-7. And finally, I would get to work criminal cases in Las Vegas...Sin City. Not to mention going to Vegas would reduce the chances of a transfer to the Western Protective Detail and if I did a good job, I could get my wish to be assigned to PPD. But in the meantime, there had to be an opening.

After about a year on the job, the boss decided it was time to shuffle the agents around and do an office realignment. To be a well-rounded investigator we had to be exposed to all criminal jurisdictions, not just one aspect. In a small or medium-sized office young agents were exposed to all of the types of the Secret Service criminal jurisdiction. But in the large offices, we were divided into different squads. I was keeping my fingers crossed for an assignment to the Counterfeit Squad. Working counterfeit cases seemed to me to be the real deal...undercover meets, controlled buys, search warrants and plenty of surveillances, busting down doors and arresting the bad guys. Fraud—white-collar crime—just seemed so bland and boring.

So, what happens? I got reassigned to the Fraud Squad! And boy was I wrong about fraud cases. The Fraud Squad boss was Assistant to the Special Agent in Charge (ATSAIC) Earl "the Pearl," the King of Fraud, and he was an incredible boss. It wasn't long after I got assigned to his squad that I heard he had just come from the Las Vegas RA, where he was the resident agent. He got promoted from Vegas to be an ATSAIC in L.A. *See? It must be true, work in Vegas, do a good job, and more to your first choice of assignments.* For "the Pearl" it was a promotion to the next higher grade; for me it could mean transfer to PPD. Or so I hoped.

In the early eighties, the Secret Service realized the future of monetary transactions was changing. Credit cards were becoming the next big thing…the news media used to run stories about how the United States was moving away from paper money into the realm of paperless financial transactions. "Someday soon," the media said, "people won't even carry currency in their pockets." There would be no need for paper money.

The US Congress was formulating a new federal statute to give federal law enforcement a tool to combat credit card fraud: Title 18 United States Code Section 1029, Unauthorized Use of an Access Device. Secret Service headquarters lobbied Congress hard for jurisdiction of this new law—after all, if the economy were moving to paperless transactions, what would we investigate? Protecting the financial system of the United States had been our primary investigative mission for decades.

The Secret Service was organized on April 14, 1865, by executive order; the last executive order signed by President Lincoln before he attended Ford's Theater for an evening performance of *Our American Cousin*. John Wilkes Booth shot President Lincoln that evening and he died the next day. A very fine investigative agency was born on April 14, 1865, though two more presidents would die from an assassin's bullet before Congress would authorize protection for the life of the president. In 1901 the Secret Service assigned agents to protect President Theodore Roosevelt, and they've been at it ever since.

During the Civil War, it was estimated that one-third of all currency in circulation was counterfeit: it was a serious threat to the country's financial freedom and economy. The Secret Service was organized to investigate counterfeiters and protect the financial system of the United States. By the 1980s the financial landscape was changing and the United States Secret Service had to change with it. Credit card fraud was becoming very popular with the criminal element. We used to always say only a fool robs a bank with a gun nowadays, all you have do is get some MasterCard or Visa account numbers and you can steal a bank blind.

At that time, credit card transactions were processed manually. A cardholder presented their credit card to the merchant and the merchant used an imprinting machine to make a copy of the card account number on a carbonized credit card receipt. One copy of the receipt for the merchant, one copy for the cardholder and a third copy to the merchant's bank to be processed through to the cardholders account for payment to the merchant. The obvious flaw in this system was that carbon copy with an account number floating around in a trash can. The "Dumpster divers" would go through trash bins behind stores and find these carbon copies casually tossed away. Now they had a valid account number to use on a counterfeit card or on the telephone to make a purchase. Today you could equate "Dumpster diver" to "computer hacker."

Credit card fraud was a new jurisdiction for the Secret Service, and at the LAFO we were gradually becoming the experts on working these cases. We were breaking new investigative ground for the Secret Service and establishing policy as we went. It was not unusual to get a call from an agent in a smaller office asking how we worked this or that type of fraud case. The conversation would start out with, "Fraud Division [at Secret Service headquarters] said you guys have worked this type of case before in L.A. and maybe you could give me some insight. What I've got here in Topeka is..."

We attacked a fraud case the only way we knew how to investigate, as agents had handled counterfeit cases for decades: develop a snitch, do some surveillance, make an undercover buy, and make an arrest.

* * *

One morning I read a message from headquarters notifying an agent at the Las Vegas RA that he had been transferred. Now was my chance, so I walked straight to Earl's office and let him know I was interested in moving to the Las Vegas RA. I went into his office thinking this is going to be a quick, short conversation. I just wanted to plant the seed. I was a little surprised when he asked me to have a seat and told me that he thought I would be an excellent candidate for that position, and what with my work ethic, I'd be a good addition to the Las Vegas RA. Then he picked up the telephone and called the special agent in charge. All I heard was Earl's side of the conversation; he had a good candidate to send to Las Vegas and he wanted to know if the SAIC had a few minutes to discuss this with him. I was trying to remain calm, but I was so excited my heart was beating out of my chest. After he hung up with the SAIC, Earl talked almost nonstop about how much I would love working in Las Vegas and when he finished our conversation with the old "I know a good real estate agent in Las Vegas" line, I knew this transfer was going to happen.

Within a couple of days I was called in to see the SAIC. As a young agent, I didn't have much interaction with the SAIC. He was the frickin' boss, for Pete's sake, and I think the most I ever said to him was "Good morning, sir" when we passed in the hallway. When I walked into his huge wood-paneled office he looked at me and asked, "Do you like to gamble?"

Gamble? "No, I don't gamble, sir," I replied. That thought never even crossed my mind.

The SAIC looked at me and said, "That's good, because gambling has ruined many a man." And the meeting was over. I was on my way to Las Vegas.

The Redhead was less than thrilled. She was a Southern California girl and her family was in Orange County. I'd been a little worried that she would balk at this move. She was well aware I wanted to get an assignment in Las Vegas. We'd only been married a couple of years and we were living in a beachfront studio apartment *in* Laguna Beach. I could roll over in the morning and look out the picture window by our bed directly at the waves rolling up the beach, just a few feet below that window...and now I was taking her to the desert: the hot, windy desert of the American Southwest and Glitter Gulch.

Chapter 3

"I Have a High-Powered Rifle"

It seemed like Tammy was getting to be a regular at our office. Donnie had her come in almost every day to make phone calls on our undercover telephone line. He had given her strict instructions to not call Roland's telephone number on her own, and if she ran into him (or Paul for that matter) *not* to initiate any meets or new check-cashing deals. Do nothing but say hello and then immediately call Donnie.

Donnie was doing everything possible to identify Roland and Paul. He'd obtained a grand jury subpoena for the telephone number Roland had written on the cocktail napkin when he met Tammy at the Four Queens. Donnie made contact with ATF, DEA, the Nevada Gaming Control Board, and even Freddie, Bernie, and Irving to see if any of these agencies knew these guys. He was coming up empty on all fronts. Without a last name it was next to impossible to positively identify Roland or Paul. The telephone company was his best bet to get Roland's real full name and some personal identifiers, like his social security number and date of birth—if he didn't lie on his telephone application, which was always a possibility. Tammy had done a decent job as an informant during the meeting at the Four Queens, especially the way she segued his romantic advances to get his telephone number, but she'd failed to get him to tell her his last name or address. Unfortunately, "Ma Bell" was taking her good old sweet time in replying to Donnie's subpoena.

* * *

As we were knee-deep in trying to pull the case together against Roland and Paul and gather some background on the two of them, we got a phone call from the LVMPD dispatch one morning reporting that a male caller had called a local telephone operator and threatened to kill President Reagan. The male caller had told an operator he had a high-powered rifle and he was going to Washington, DC, to kill the President. Before he hung up, he was kind enough to tell the operator that his name was William Lee.

Protective intelligence cases, what we referred to as threat cases, were our number one criminal investigative priority. When the Secret Service became aware of a threat against the President, everything stopped and all our attention was devoted to those investigations. Roland and Paul would have to wait: William Lee was about to take up a lot of my time.

LVMPD said the call had originated from a pay phone in a local bar on Maryland Parkway, not far from downtown Vegas. I grabbed Donnie and we headed to the address the PD dispatcher gave us.

The bar was a typical Las Vegas neighborhood watering hole; it was dark and smelled of cigarettes. When we arrived it was mid-morning and the place was pretty much empty. There was an old guy sitting at the bar playing video poker and some gal that looked close to eighty, sitting at a slot machine by the front door, cigarette dangling from the corner of her mouth as she robotically pulled the handle.

William was easy to spot. He was the drunk sitting all alone at a table against the wall. He had on a dirty, powder blue sport coat with a yellowish shirt that had at one time probably been white. He looked like a down-and-out banker, like someone who had once actually known how to dress himself properly at some point in his past. I noticed he didn't have on socks, but what appeared to be nylons under his pants. Pantyhose.

He was a white male, a very white male; he could have used a few hours sitting in the sun. He was about thirty-five, red hair, clean-shaven, and stank of bourbon. His fingers were stained with nicotine and his fingernails were painted with flesh-colored nail polish. It was what the Redhead would have referred to as a "very poor manicure"; to me it looked like he had one too many Jack Daniel's before he put the polish on.

It wasn't hard to convince William to come with us to our office. Once we told him he wasn't under arrest and that we just wanted to talk to him about the telephone call, he willingly got up from the table and walked out to Donnie's sedan with us.

Secret Service agents are given a huge responsibly. If you are the case agent on a criminal investigation, you are in charge, you take the case where it needs to go, make the arrest, and get a conviction. If you are given an advance assignment for a "protectee," you come up with a plan to secure the venue. Of course, supervisors are involved in all of this, but believe me, US Secret Service agents are leaders and self-starters and agents are expected to get it right without much input from a supervisor. Bosses don't have time to hold your hand.

One of the biggest responsibilities is making a determination if a person is really a threat to the President of the United States. And that is one call that you have to get right, because believe me, there is a lot of scrutiny of a Protective Intelligence investigative report by every agent up the chain, through the chain, and near the chain of command.

Donnie and I interviewed the crap out of William; we were trying our best to get inside his head and see what he was really thinking. Would he really try to kill the President of the United States? We spent a few hours in the interview room with him and it became apparent that William had an issue, that's for sure. He had what we'd call a gender identification issue these days.

William was cooperative during our interview, a little drunk, no doubt, but he was cooperative nonetheless. He waived his Miranda rights and admitted right up front that he made the phone call to the operator and told her he had a high-powered rifle and he was going to DC to kill Reagan. He told us he wasn't really going to do it, it just seemed like something to say at the time.

He consented to a search of his apartment and we took him home. Donnie and I searched the place and found nothing of investigative interest. It appeared he lived with a woman—dresses and high heels in the closet and makeup on the dresser. But he didn't; he lived alone.

I called over to the US Attorney's office and they declined to prosecute William for threatening to kill the President due to his inebriated state of mind when he made the call.

I wrote my investigative report and sent it up the chain. I made the preliminary determination that William was not a threat to the President, at the time. I wasn't sure if he was crazy or just an alcoholic; but he definitely had some mental issues. During the course of my investigation, I learned he was originally from Los Angeles and he had once worked for an insurance company. Inquiries with the mental health facilities in Nevada and California proved to be negative—he had never been admitted or treated for mental illness.

The problem with some of these guys who were teetering between the sane world and the insane world was that they craved attention. And it was no different for William. Now I was his best friend, or at least someone who would come and have a conversation with him when he was lonely. Within three weeks, he felt the need to talk with me again. In William's alcohol-fueled brain, he figured the best way for me to show up at his doorstep would be to pick up the phone, dial "0," and tell the operator he was going to kill President Reagan.

William upped the ante this time. He told the operator he had an airline ticket, 158 rounds of ammunition, and he was going to Washington, DC, to kill the President.

The Beaver went with me to William's apartment and we interviewed him once again. William was drunk and dressed exactly the same as the first day I met him. His fingernails still had the shitty manicure of flesh-colored nail polish and he wore the pantyhose under his trousers.

But William was a just another drunk craving attention. I read him the riot act and told him to sober up, stop calling the operator and threatening the President. The US Attorney once again declined to prosecute him and I didn't have an issue with that decision. I updated my investigative report for headquarters and continued looking into his background for any signs he actually might make good on his threat.

William behaved himself for a few months and I kept tabs on him, while continuing the investigation into his background and mental history. I had to send requests to other field offices in cities where he'd previously lived and worked. I interviewed some folks who knew him in Las Vegas. His neighbors said he was very quiet, but they didn't know him well. The landlord said he paid his rent on time and never caused any trouble. All of this background information was extremely important in order for me to make a final recommendation to headquarters as to whether or not William was a genuine threat to the life of the President.

Unfortunately, William's mental state continued to deteriorate. After about sixty days he completely flipped his lid. This time he dialed 9-1-1 and said he was going to do it...he was going to kill President Reagan. After getting the call from LVMPD dispatch, Donnie and I went over to his apartment. It was time for William to visit the psychiatric ward at University Hospital and it was time for him to go to jail.

William answered our knock on his apartment door and invited us in; he was in pretty bad shape. He'd been hitting the Jim Beam hard and reeked of bourbon. He wore the same outfit; dirty sport coat, tie, and pantyhose under his trousers. *Who sits around their frickin' apartment in that get-up all day?* His fingernails were still painted with the flesh-colored nail polish, but now he wore red lipstick, a drunken outline of his lips and way too much red rouge on his cheeks.

We took him to the psychiatric ward and dropped him off for a forty-eight-hour mental health examination. I went to the US Attorney's office and wrote out a complaint for his arrest.

I ended up indicting William for three counts of violation of Title 18 United States Code Section 871, Threats Against the President. I had just made my first arrest of someone threatening to kill the President of the United States.

William was held without bail and the psychiatric report by the doctor at University Hospital wasn't good, but it wasn't bad either. William wasn't "insane"; the psychiatrist stated William exhibited "paranoid schizophrenic" tendencies due to alcohol abuse. *No shit, I could have come up with that diagnosis.*

William pleaded guilty to one count of the three-count indictment. A federal judge sentenced William to six months confinement at a federal treatment facility to provide him the opportunity to conquer his alcoholism and five years probation. William was unable to conquer his demons and within three years his probation was revoked and the judge sentenced him to eighteen months in a federal medical treatment facility in Springfield, Missouri.

I always wondered about William…did he get drunk and dress up like a woman, or did he dress up like a woman and then get drunk? And I'm sure the answer to that question was the reason he ended up in Springfield.

* * *

In between my waltzing around with William and working on his background information, Tammy finally made contact with Roland and he graciously put her in direct contact with Paul. I was listening in on her recorded telephone call placed from our undercover telephone. Roland acted as if he and Tammy were old friends. This was odd, but I guess that's what drugs do to your mind, and it was a big mistake by Roland. We couldn't have hoped for a better break in this case, because now Tammy would be dealing directly with the suspect who'd made the counterfeit driver's license, and we wouldn't have to work through Roland hoping he'd make an introduction.

Donnie immediately had Tammy place a recorded telephone call to the number Roland gave her for Paul. She told Paul her boyfriend had a check to cash but he didn't have identification to match the name on the check. Paul said he wanted to speak to the boyfriend and Tammy handed me the telephone. Paul didn't suspect a thing and offered to alter my driver's license to match the name on the check. Under the Federal False Identification Statute, an altered driver's license is considered a counterfeit driver's license. We were hoping Paul would manufacture a new counterfeit driver's license like he'd done for Tammy the night she was arrested, but Donnie, who was listening in, gave me the thumbs-up and he had that look on his face like "let's get this case over with."

I asked Paul how much this altered driver's license would cost me and he said, "One hundred bucks, kiddo. What's the amount on the check?"

We had "spurious" US Treasury checks in the office safe. Headquarters issued these checks specifically for this type of undercover deal. The only problem was I didn't know what the amounts of the "spurious" checks were. I said to Paul, "Well, uh," and I looked up at Donnie and kind of shrugged my shoulders. Donnie was holding up eight fingers and nodding. "Eight hundred bucks," I said and Donnie smiled real big.

"Okay…a hundred bucks up front and a hundred bucks when we cash the check." Perfect incriminating verbal evidence right out from the crook's mouth!

"I live over near Twain and Swenson," he said, and he gave me his address. "Come on over, kiddo, and we'll get this going."

I looked at Donnie for some direction. We needed time to get the surveillance teams set up to provide cover for me. Donnie pointed to his watch and held up four fingers. I glanced at my watch; it was a little after two in he afternoon. "I'll swing by about four o'clock," I said.

"Bring the check and don't forget your driver's license," Paul said.

We'd had undercover Nevada driver's licenses issued to all three of us, so I had a Nevada driver's license he could alter. And the "spurious" checks were all made out with gender-neutral names.

The only problem was of the five "spurious" checks in the evidence vault; none of them were in the amount of eight hundred dollars. The closest was seven hundred and seventy-five dollars and it would have to do.

Donnie got the surveillance team together with Beaver and two ATF agents. I wore a tape recorder to record my conversations with Paul and a UHF transmitter so Donnie could monitor the conversation while I was in the apartment. Paul's apartment complex was behind the Desert Inn Hotel and Casino, and while I was getting wired up, Beaver and one of the ATF agents went over to keep tabs on Paul.

Donnie and I tested all the recording equipment and the transmitter. I grabbed my Smith and Wesson Model 60, off-duty revolver and stuck it in my left cowboy boot. I had the tape recorder taped to my right ankle, with the microphone wire running up my leg. We taped the microphone to my chest and I secured the UHF transmitter to my lower stomach, that no-man's-land between your belt line and your pecker, the UHF transmitter's microphone was taped under my beltline. I felt like a frickin' walking sound studio; but Donnie looked me over and did a quick pat down and said he couldn't see or feel the wires or equipment. Off I went in my IROC-Z to meet Paul. Donnie and the second ATF agent headed over to the apartment complex and set up where Donnie could see the front door of the apartment, while Beaver watched the back.

Paul met me at the door and let me in. The apartment was rank and smelled of old socks and urine. There was a girl sitting in the kitchen, she looked early twenties. She was fiddling with something on the small kitchen table, but I couldn't quite see what she was up to and she barely acknowledged me. Paul had me follow him down the hallway to a bedroom. My gut tightened up a little, as I was fearful a pat down was coming. I was talking up a storm, being as accurate as to my location in the apartment and what we were doing so Donnie and the "cavalry" would know exactly where I was and who was in there in case I needed help.

I'm not a tall guy by any means, I'm just shy of six foot, but this guy was short. His head came up to my sternum. He wore thick glasses, had slicked-back jet-black hair with dandruff flakes, a dingy white tank-top T-shirt, and black trousers. He looked like he'd just stepped out of a 1950s gangster movie. Plus, he had an East Coast tough-guy accent, with a deep voice. A hand-rolled cigarette dangled from his lips. He squinted to keep the smoke out of his eyes. And skinny; I could see the outline of his ribs through the worn fabric of his T-shirt. His bare biceps…well, he didn't have any bicep muscles that I could see. I started to relax; *if this guy starts any shit with me, I'll kill him if I blow too hard on him!*

The bedroom really stunk; I was trying not to breathe too deeply. He was standing way too close for comfort so I stepped back a little. "What's a matter," he growled.

"I'm tryin' to quit smoking, man!"

He laughed, "Yeah, me too!" That broke the ice and he asked me in that deep, smoky Jersey gangster accent, "Watcha got?"

I pulled the Treasury check out of my back pocket and held it up for him. "Nice," he said. "A Ben Franklin up front and a Ben Franklin when we cash it. That's the deal. Let me see the license." I handed him my undercover Nevada driver's license. He took a big, deep drag of the cigarette, "This'll work just fine. And I'm going with you to cash the check. You don't leave my sight."

"Hey sure," I told him, "No problem." I followed Paul back into his living room. Paul sat down at a desk against the wall and opened the top right side drawer. From my angle I couldn't see into the desk drawer, but he fished around and pulled out an X-Acto knife. He had a bright desk lamp attached to the desk with a clamp and he put half sleeves on his arms, the ones like an accountant wore in an old movie. I was half expecting him to pull out a green shaded visor to put on his head to finish the ensemble.

Paul had a typewriter, colored pens, stencils, and all kinds of shit on that desk. Plus, he liked to talk while he worked, so I let him go on and on about how skilled he was at making counterfeit driver's licenses. I walked over and stood by his desk and watched him work. I made a half-assed attempt at a narration of what he was doing, for the amusement of Donnie out in the car and, more importantly, the tape a jury might hear someday down the road, if this case went to trial.

Paul was very accommodating, answering my inquisitive questions about the finer points of altering a driver's license. All of a sudden it seemed like we were best buddies; he'd completely let his guard down and wasn't questioning me about anything. He was focused on altering that driver's license. "First, I gotta pull back the lamination so I can change the name," he told me, "Then the hard part is getting the lamination stuck back on the front so it doesn't look like it's been fucked with." *Keep talking, Paul, just keep talking...and pull that jail door shut behind you.*

Paul scraped the name off my undercover driver's license and put it in the typewriter. He looked at the name on the check, "Pat Thomas," he looked puzzled. "Pat," he said again, "That's a girl's name."

"Patrick," I quickly said. "Put Patrick Thomas on the license."

"Oh yeah," he mumbled, "Oh yeah, oh yeah...perfect, perfect, perfect."

While I was getting as much incriminating evidence out of Paul's mouth as he would provide, I glanced over at the girl in the kitchen. She was shooting a syringe full of heroin in between her toes on her left foot. *Wonderful. Come on, Paul; let's get this done so I can get out of here.*

Suddenly, the front door opened and I felt like I'd stopped breathing. Roland walked in with two young ladies. Two rough-looking young ladies; two very drugged up young ladies.

Roland didn't say shit to Paul. Paul didn't say shit to Roland. I didn't know what to say to anybody. *Come on, Paul, finish up, buddy...Let's go!*

Roland and his girls plopped down on the old, smelly couch. Finally, Paul says to Roland, "Today is payday," and he chuckles. Roland got up and walked over toward the desk. He stood behind Paul and put his hands on Paul's shoulders, as he peeked over to look at Paul's work.

I looked over at the couch and one of the girls was setting up a laboratory on the coffee table. *Great, more dope.* Roland asked Paul "What's the take?"

Paul said, "Two hundred bucks, baby." Roland gave me a high five. No shit! I made a mental note to take a hot soapy shower after this deal.

Roland rejoined the drug party on the couch and casually asked if I wanted a hit.

"No, thanks, pal, my probation officer frowns on that stuff."

Finally, Paul pushed his chair back from the desk and held up the shittiest-looking altered driver's license I had ever seen. The font he used to change my undercover name from "Henry Detmer" to the "Patrick Thomas" was obviously way off and the ink was darker than the original. It was a piece of shit, but hey, Title 18 United States Code Section 1028 doesn't say it has to be a good counterfeit identification document; it just has to be counterfeit. "Perfect!" I exclaimed, as I stuck the driver's license in my pocket. "Let's go get paid! I'm going to Acapulco!"

Paul looked up at me as the smoke from his cigarette stung his squinty eyes, "Don't ya owe me something?"

"Oh yeah," I said and I pulled out a hundred-dollar bill from my front jeans pocket and gave it to him. "Here you go, Paul, one hundred dollars."

Paul walked over to an easy chair and started putting on his shoes. I walked over to the door and cracked it open just a hair. I could see Donnie, Beaver, and the ATF agents on the stoop. Paul jumped up and walked toward the door to follow me out. As I opened the door, Donnie and the guys burst in. I slipped outside and reached down to turn off the tape recorder. The Beaver stepped out of the apartment and handcuffed me. He took me off to one side and acted like he was reading me my Miranda Warning. Donnie and one of the ATF agents led the handcuffed Roland out of the apartment and put him in the back of Donnie's car. The other ATF agent followed behind with a handcuffed Paul. Two LVMPD officers, who Donnie had called when he heard the conversation about the heroin, walked in and arrested the three girls for possession. All in all, it was a good day.

Believe it or not, these guys decided to go to trial on this case. Tammy was the star witness and did a fine job on direct examination by the AUSA, and she held her ground on cross-examination by the two defense counsels. They, of course, tried to paint a picture for the jury that she'd set up the defendants, that she approached Roland and asked him to get her a counterfeit driver's license, and that Roland and Paul had refused to help her, but that she kept pestering them until they agreed to "just help her out."

She, of course, denied that any of that was true and on re-direct examination the AUSA was able to reestablishing her credibility for the jury. Like all trials with a snitch, it would come down to who the jury believed was telling the truth—Tammy and a Secret Service agent or Roland and Paul.

When I testified, the AUSA had me introduce the tape recordings of my conversation with Paul on the telephone, setting up the meeting at the apartment. Then we played the tape recording of the meeting in Paul's apartment. We introduced the altered driver's license, the "spurious" Treasury check, and the one-hundred-dollar bill I gave Paul into evidence for the jury. On cross-examination, Paul's attorney tried to convince the jury that I'd entrapped Paul by telling him to change the name on my undercover driver's license to "Patrick Thomas," trying anything to put doubt into the mind of at least one juror.

In his re-direct of me on the witness stand and again in his closing statement, the AUSA was able to clearly define entrapment for the jury and establish legal precedent that my suggestion for the name on the driver's license was not even close to entrapment.

The jury deliberated for less than an hour and came back with a guilty verdict on all counts of the indictment. At his sentencing, Paul's lawyer argued for leniency from the judge: poor old Paul had AIDS. But, the US district court judge was not buying it and sentenced Paul to five years imprisonment and Roland to four years.

Chapter 4

An Easy Mark

A irline ticket fraud was big business back in the eighties. This
was in the old days when you could buy and sell airline tickets
from one person to another; the name on the ticket didn't matter.
You could buy a ticket on United Airlines for a flight on January 1
and if you didn't use that ticket on United on January 1, you could
use it on American (or any airline) and use it on any date after
January 1. It was a crazy system and it was ripe for the fraudsters
to get involved. And boy, did they ever.

Back then; some large corporations had credit accounts with
the major airlines for their employees to charge airline tickets and
hotel rooms while on business travel. If a crook obtained of one
of these account numbers, he could travel the world, bill his hotel
to that account, eat all the room service he wanted, drink all the
champagne he could hold and order up a limo to take him to

the airport for his next adventure. The bad guys could use this corporate account number for only a short period of time until the corporation reconciled their travel expenses against employee travel. But in the meantime, the crook could live the high life for at least thirty days on that stolen corporate account number.

I have always said all criminals, especially fraudsters and counterfeiters, come to Las Vegas at some point. They come to Vegas to continue their scams or to spend the cash they've ripped off from banks, the government or the innocent victim. Either way, eventually, they show up in Sin City. Donnie's mantra was that when you work a fraud case, you could bet the suspect is not who he says he is and it is not the first time he has done it. Both are absolute truths about scam artists.

One sunny April morning, I got a telephone call from a lady named Missy who owned a small one-man travel agency on Rainbow Boulevard in Las Vegas. She had a very interesting and complicated story to tell me. Missy said she had been dealing with a very wealthy client for the past few days, a Mr. Martin Malcheski. He had contacted her travel agency and purchased numerous first class airline tickets and also had her make reservations at four and five star hotels all over the United States. She said she thought he was a high roller, a common occurrence in Las Vegas, and she thought she had hit the mother lode when he kept using her small business as his personal travel agent. She was raking in the commissions and he was scamming the crap out of her. All fraudsters need an easy mark and unfortunately, Missy took the bait and swallowed the hook.

Martin Malcheski's real name was Mark Matthews. Matthews was a credit card fraud master, who had been arrested and convicted of credit card fraud and incarcerated in a federal penitentiary. Matthews had escaped and was on the run from the US Marshals. You'd think if you were lucky enough to escape from prison, you'd lay low, get a job, and try to blend into society; you know, move to

Iowa and get a job at the local feed store. But not Matthews, he was addicted to the easy money that comes from bilking travel agents with stolen credit card account numbers. Of course, Missy didn't know that at the time, and I didn't know it, either, until I started the investigation.

Once Martin realized Missy was his "easy mark," like any good con man and scam artist he used every opportunity he had to take advantage of her. According to Missy, Martin had called her just two days ago from the Las Vegas Airport saying he was on his way to the Big Island of Hawaii and at the last minute decided to make a one night stop in Las Vegas for some R&R. Unfortunately, according to Martin, the travel agent he'd used for this trip was an incompetent boob and had totally dropped the ball. His hotel reservations at Caesar's Palace were made for the wrong day, and the hotel was telling him they had no rooms available. Martin told her he was still at the airport and was at a loss as to where he could find an acceptable hotel room for the night.

Missy tried her contacts at all the big hotels and she wasn't having any luck finding him a room. It was getting late in the day, so she did what any fine, upstanding travel agent would do for a high-roller client: She offered him a room at her house for the night. Not only would he spend the night at her house, but she also paid for a limo to go out to the airport and bring him directly to her home: bringing this escaped prisoner to the home she shared with her husband and two small children. Fortunately for Missy and her young family, he was just a con man and not a pedophile or a crazy serial killer.

Yesterday morning Missy paid for Martin's limo ride back to the Las Vegas airport so he could catch his flight to Kona on the Big Island of Hawaii. And her husband loaned Martin his three hundred dollar Rosetta Stone Spanish learning course, because Martin wanted to learn Spanish for his upcoming trip to San Juan!

That's all he took from their house, but he stole tens of thousands of dollars in airline tickets and hotel rooms that Missy was left to pay for. I guess she got lucky.

Missy told me Martin telephoned her after he arrived at the Hyatt Hotel in Kona, Hawaii, to thank her for her hospitality during his short layover in Las Vegas. Martin told her he would be in Hawaii for a few days and he was extremely happy with her professionalism; she was the best travel agent he'd ever used. He told her he would be calling her again for more airline tickets and hotel reservations once he had an itinerary for his next travel assignment.

Missy told me American Express had just telephoned her and told her the American Express account number she had been charging all of Martin's tickets to was stolen and Martin was not authorized to use that account number. She was in a panic, a complete utter panic.

* * *

About a month before Missy called me, I had been working an airline ticket fraud scam that involved an unknown suspect using the alias Marcus Hanes. Dennis Bowery, a marketing manager for a large local travel agency in Las Vegas, called me and related that Mr. Hanes had defrauded their agency for ten thousand dollars over a five-day period.

Hanes was using Bowery's travel agency to purchase airline tickets for his personal first class travel all over the United States. Hanes used a United Airlines issued corporate account number for the tickets and United Airlines had eventually notified the business the account number had been compromised. The business contacted Bowery and advised him all charges by Marcus Hanes were unauthorized and fraudulent. As a matter of fact, the victim business had no employees named Marcus Hanes.

Bowery told me that Hanes had telephoned the travel agency the day before and ordered a prepaid first class airline ticket in the name Marcus Hanes for travel from Seattle to Honolulu to Los Angeles. Mr. Bowery said Hanes asked for the ticket to be sent Federal Express to the Four Seasons Olympic Hotel in Seattle and he would pick up the ticket when he checked in later that day. He told the travel agent that he would be calling back between one and two o'clock that afternoon to order some more tickets.

One thing I learned working in the LAFO fraud squad was that the masters of these cons could and would disappear into thin air in a heartbeat. You have to remember this was the 1980s... the personal computer was still evolving and false identification was easy to make and use. There was no Internet. Shit, there was no e-mail or voicemail! A cop, much less a young cashier at a casino cash cage, wouldn't know the difference between a Delaware driver's license and a French passport. If it looked official, you were good to go. So I had to jump on this one and I had to get moving fast. I needed help and I needed it now.

I looked at my watch; it was eleven thirty in the morning. *Shit! Not much time to pull this caper together.* I ran into the Beaver's office to fill him in and before I could open my mouth he asked, "Where are we going to lunch today?" The Beaver and I had been on a crusade to find the best cheeseburger in Las Vegas—and we'd found some tasty ones already, but not today. Well, not right now, we might have time for a cheeseburger later this afternoon...

I grabbed Beaver and we hustled down the hall to see the boss. I told the boss I was thinking we could get the Seattle FO to do a controlled delivery of the airline ticket at the Four Seasons Hotel. When Marcus Hanes checked in and claimed the ticket, they could arrest him. In the meantime, I'd go by the travel agency and tape the incoming call from the suspect when he called to order more airline tickets. I figured that way we have the suspect on tape admitting he bought the airline ticket with the stolen account number. Then I would get the ticket from the local travel agency and I would send it overnight express to the Seattle FO. All they had to do was make a controlled delivery and make the arrest. *Bada-bing, Bada-boom!* We got him!

The boss said he would call Seattle and see if they could assist us with the controlled delivery and make the arrest. The Beaver gathered up the recording equipment to tape the incoming call and we drove to Bowery's travel agency.

By the time we got the recorder set up on one of the travel agent's desk phone and briefed the receptionist to transfer any calls from Mr. Hanes to Sherry's desk, it was close to one o'clock. Beaver sat down at Sherry's desk, waiting to play travel agent with Mr. Hanes and we waited and waited. Finally at about two o'clock, Mr. Hanes called in. The Beaver was a good bullshitter and when Mr. Hanes balked at speaking with "Bob" instead of Sherry, well the Beaver just jumped in there with the old, "I'm so sorry Mr. Hanes, Sherry had a family emergency yesterday and I'm filling in for her today."

Hanes claimed he was in Atlanta and he would arrive in Seattle later that night. "Bob" apologized to Hanes and explained that with Sherry's quick departure from the office, he had dropped the ball and didn't get the ticket to Federal Express in time for a delivery today. "Bob" said he was extremely embarrassed about his faux pas and he would personally take the package to the FedEx office to ensure delivery for tomorrow morning to the Four Seasons Hotel in Seattle. "Oh, and one more thing Mr. Hanes…please accept two free upgrade certificates on United Airlines as compensation for any pain and suffering you may have experienced due to this delay."

During the conversation, I was sitting next to Beaver and I had an earpiece so I could hear every word. I had to clamp my hand over my mouth because I was dying laughing at Beaver's Mr. Peabody voice. The Beaver looked at me, winked, and asked

Hanes if he could possibly trouble him to please verify the credit account number the ticket should be charged to. "I sure don't want any more foul-ups on your travel plans." Hanes gave the Beaver the account number and "Bob" ended the call. The Beaver came through with an awesome performance; I called him Bob for the rest of the week.

Bowery gave me the fraudulently purchased airline ticket so I could overnight it to Seattle, and the Beaver and I headed back to the office with the incriminating tape. On the way, we stopped at a neighborhood casino near Nellis Boulevard and East Desert Inn Road to try out their cheeseburger. Just as we were digging into lunch, my pager went off. I looked at the number on the display and saw it was the boss's extension, so I went to the pay phone and called in. The boss said he spoke with the Seattle FO and I should call Agent Jim Henderson in Seattle to fill him in.

Back at the office I called Jim in Seattle. He was a little hesitant about the controlled delivery; he kept telling me he would have to run it by the US Attorney's office in Seattle. He said the US Attorney in Seattle was not a big proponent of probable cause (PC) arrests. I stressed the urgency of the matter. "Jim, if we are going to catch this guy, we have to act on it tomorrow." Jim said he'd call the duty AUSA in Seattle and get back to me.

I was just a young agent, with just over three years on the job, and the US Attorney in Las Vegas had completely spoiled the agents in the Las Vegas RA. We were blessed with an extremely aggressive Chief of the Criminal Division at the US Attorney's office in Las Vegas. He never turned down our requests for a PC arrest. His staff in the Criminal Division was just as aggressive and it made our job that much more fun, knowing that when we rolled out at zero-dark thirty for a duty call on the Strip, we could count on the duty AUSA to back us up and put the bad guys in jail. After my first few years in Vegas, the chief told us we had carte blanche to make PC arrests.

"Don't even bother waking up my duty AUSA," he said. "Just make the arrest and call us first thing in the morning."

When I look back on those days at the Las Vegas RA, especially after my career moved on and I worked criminal cases in other states with other US Attorneys, I'm awed at the cooperation the US Attorney gave us in Vegas. Donnie, the Beaver, and I made so many PC arrests; I took it for granted that I could arrest anyone if I had the PC. But Vegas was different in that respect; the vast majority of US Attorney's offices would *not* allow an agent to make a PC arrest. I had to hope Jim could convince the Seattle AUSA to approve Hanes's arrest.

Jim finally called me back and said his duty AUSA had turned down the request for a PC arrest. No fraud had been committed in Seattle and they refused to prosecute the case. Or some such bullshit. "No problem," I told Jim. "I'll get a John Doe arrest warrant here in Vegas." I told Jim the ticket was already on its way to Seattle and was guaranteed delivery to his attention by ten thirty the next morning. I told him I would fax the arrest warrant to him in Seattle later that day. I hoped anyway. I called T.J., the criminal chief at the US Attorney's office. "Bring your case file and come on over."

T.J. and I sat down and went over the case. "No problem," he said. "Let's get this guy." T.J. wasn't crazy about getting a John Doe arrest warrant without the certainty that Hanes would accept delivery of the ticket. He was worried he'd have to take up court time to get the warrant squashed if we didn't find the guy. "Write up the affidavit, with the last paragraph saying Hanes accepted delivery of the ticket at the Four Seasons Hotel," he said. "I'll make an appointment with the duty US magistrate judge for late tomorrow morning and have your Seattle agents call you as soon as he takes receipt and signs for the airline ticket. Have them keep a surveillance on Hanes, we'll get the warrant signed and then they can take him down." *What a great plan! Thank you, T.J.*

I called Jim in Seattle and told him the plan...and he was still hesitating, "Well, I don't know if we have enough guys in the office tomorrow to do a surveillance." *Are you kidding me? Holy shit, help me out here, Jimbo!* It was officially time to get the boss involved in this one.

The boss got on the telephone with the ASAIC in Seattle and, wouldn't you know it, Seattle suddenly had enough agents to cover the surveillance. Finally! Now, I just needed Hanes to show up at the Four Seasons Hotel.

Jim called me the next morning and said he had the airline ticket and they were going over to the Four Seasons to make the controlled delivery. I called T.J. and went over to stand by at his office and wait for the call from Jim.

We waited and we waited. No word from Seattle. T.J. called the US magistrate's office and cancelled our appointment. "No problem," T.J. said. "If they call you later today, the magistrate's clerk said he had an open calendar this afternoon and he could see us to sign the warrant anytime before four." So, I went back to my office to wait it out.

Jim finally called and said Hanes had not checked into the Four Seasons last night or that day. He was sending the airline ticket back to me. Hanes had escaped the dragnet. *Shit!* I didn't have much hope that I would ever identify and arrest this guy.

A few weeks later, I happened to be on the telephone with the West Coast region agent at Fraud Division and I mentioned the Hanes caper. "Marcus Hanes," the headquarters agent said to me. "That name sounds real familiar. Stand by a minute." I could hear him talking to another agent in his office. He came back on the phone and said, "Call Agent Roger Hood in Indianapolis. Roger has been working a very similar airline ticket scam in Indiana."

I called Hood and he told me about a credit card fraud case he'd been working in Indianapolis; his suspect was a guy using the name

Marcus Hanes. *Whoa, excellent!* He went on to say he had tentatively identified Hanes as Mark Matthews, who was an escapee from a federal penitentiary. He put me in contact with a US Probation officer (PO) in Indianapolis, who was looking for Matthews.

The PO said Matthews had escaped from a federal facility in December of 1988 and there was an outstanding warrant for his arrest. It was now February 1989; he'd been on the run for about ninety days. The PO mailed me a photograph of Matthews and I obtained a copy of the warrant through the National Crime Information Center (NCIC). Now I just needed to find this guy...

* * *

I'm listening to Missy tell me this complicated story of being ripped off by "Malcheski," and suddenly the lightbulb went on in my head—Marcus Hanes! *Holy shit. Hanes...Malcheski...It's got to be Matthews."*

I grabbed my Hanes case folder and drove over to see Missy at her travel agency. I obtained copies of evidence from her records documenting the credit card fraud and told her that if Martin called her again to act normal and find out what he needed. If he wanted more tickets, just take the information like you normally would. We didn't want him to get suspicious at this point.

I had Missy listen to the tape recording of the Beaver speaking with Hanes that I'd recorded months before. She said the caller's voice sounded a lot like Martin, but she couldn't say for certain it was Malcheski. I then showed her a photo spread I had prepared of six similar-looking white males. One of the six photos was Mark Matthews. I asked her to tell me if she recognized the man she knew as Martin, the man who stayed at her house that one night a few days ago. With no hesitation she pointed directly at the photo of Matthews and said, "That's him."

"Are you sure?" I ask.

"Oh yes," she said to me. "That's the son of a bitch!" When Missy and I were on the telephone earlier that day she had been panicky, thinking of how she had been taken advantage of and realizing "Martin" had scammed her out of tens of thousands of dollars. Now that she saw justice was around the corner, she became angry. A very typical reaction for victims of crime. I had her sign and date the photo spread.

I jumped into my IROC-Z and broke numerous traffic laws getting back to the office. I did not run any red lights, but I came damn close.

I called T.J. and filled him in and he was as excited as I was. T.J. asked me to contact the Secret Service office in Honolulu to see if they could arrest Matthews at the Hyatt in Kona on the outstanding escape warrant. "No sweat," I told T.J. "The boss is on the telephone with Honolulu as we speak." T.J. wanted me to draft an affidavit for an arrest warrant on the violations we had in Las Vegas. A lot of US attorneys would have ended the case right then and there; the suspect was in custody (or would be soon) and the federal courts would sentence him on the escape charge. Case closed. But not T.J. "I'm gonna extradite Matthews to Las Vegas and we will hammer him for good." T.J. was an agent's attorney; he loved prosecuting criminals to the fullest extent of the law.

Agent Chuck Stubbe, one of my old LAFO buddies was now in Honolulu, and he was more than willing to hunt down Matthews on the Big Island. He and another Honolulu agent jumped on the first plane to Kona and had a local cop pick them up at the airport.

Chuck called me later that day and told me they were able to identify Matthews and arrest him as he sat by the hotel swimming pool drinking a piña colada. Chuck was able to get a written consent from Matthews to search his hotel room, and they recovered numerous credit card account numbers and airline ticket receipts.

Chuck said the US magistrate in Honolulu held Matthews in custody without bail, and he also served my warrant on Matthews. He said the Honolulu AUSA was talking to T.J. about handling all the court proceedings from the District of Nevada in the US District Court of Hawaii, which legally could be done if Matthews agreed to waive extradition to Nevada, since both jurisdictions are US district courts. I called T.J. "Are you planning on letting Honolulu handle our case?"

"Absolutely not," said T.J. "No way will I allow Matthews to enjoy the balmy breezes of Hawaii. He scammed Las Vegas travel agents and he will face justice in a Las Vegas courtroom." That's why Donnie, the Beaver, and I loved this guy so much: he was a frickin' tiger of a prosecutor.

T.J. and I indicted Matthews for five counts of violation of Title 18 United States Code Section 1029. The hammer was about to come down on Mr. Matthews and his credit card fraud endeavors and it was coming down in the hot, dusty Great American Desert.

About a month later, Matthews was sitting in the Clark County Jail awaiting trial on our indictment. T.J. called me one day and said Matthews's attorney was considering accepting the government's offer in exchange for a guilty plea; but the defense attorney wanted to try one thing to question the photo spread identification Missy had made on Matthews. It was his last hope. If Missy picked Matthews out of a police lineup, he'd recommend Matthews take the guilty plea.

T.J. told me to make sure I let the defense attorney pick the other inmates for the lineup. "Is he that dumb?" I asked T.J.

"Oh yeah," T.J. laughed, "He's that dumb."

I contacted the watch commander at the jail and made arrangements for a line up. The defense attorney did exactly what T.J. thought he would do and as the jailers paraded a group of inmates into the room, he starting selecting this guy, then that guy. I just stood back and let him go. That brilliant federal public defender just put the last nail in Matthews coffin; by having him pick the other five inmates for the lineup, he ruined any chance of having the line-up thrown out of court as biased toward the defendant. Any argument that the other five inmates did not resemble Matthews would be a moot point.

Missy, the defense attorney, and I were standing behind the one-way glass in the lineup room when they opened the curtain. The sergeant had the six inmates face forward, turn to the left, and turn to the right. He then had them face forward again. Missy looked at the six inmates and without hesitation said, "Number two. That's him. That's the man I know as Martin Malcheski."

Matthews pleaded guilty to counts one through four of the indictment. He served over seventeen years in a federal penitentiary and was released in 2007.

Chapter 5

Lucky Cargill

One Friday evening as I was just pulling into my driveway and thinking it would be a good night to sit in the hot tub with the Redhead and sip on a beer, my Motorola radio squawked to life. It was Donnie and he wanted to know if I could give him a phone call at the office ASAP. I turned off the ignition and headed into the house and the closest phone.

I was the duty agent during this particular week and I'd been hoping all day the frickin' telephone wouldn't ring that night. It had been a busy week, lots of middle-of-the-night duty calls, and I just wanted to relax, watch a little baseball, and sleep all weekend. We didn't have cell phones in those days. They might have existed, but the Secret Service, at least the Secret Service in Las Vegas, sure didn't have any! We had pagers that would send out an audible beep when you were getting a message. They didn't even vibrate; they just beeped. Therefore, we referred to them as our "beepers." As I walked toward the kitchen phone, I looked at my beeper to see if I'd missed a call. Nothing. That was a good sign.

I was a little on the defensive side when I called Donnie at the office. I thought he must have gotten a duty call that I'd missed and I figured he'd be pissed off. We only had three agents in Las Vegas (and the boss) and we rotated the duty agent assignment from Monday morning to Monday morning; so every third week you were the duty agent for the office. It was a huge pain in the ass; the unwritten rule was, "Don't make any plans" during your turn on duty—not dinner plans, not going-to-the-movies plans, not friends or family in town so let's do something fun plans. If you did, you were guaranteed they would be disrupted.

The duty agent usually caught all new cases when it was their turn. The damn telephone was constantly ringing, it was unusual to make it through the night without a call, and not all calls were important. But you had to answer them. It didn't bother me so much, because I loved rolling out in the middle of the night to a casino with one in custody. That was too much fun! But the Redhead wasn't so crazy about getting woken up every night by the ringing of the telephone. You can't blame her, she had a regular job, what I called a "real people job." Me, I was just a Secret Service agent doing my part to clean up the streets of Vegas.

Casinos would call at all hours of the night to get us to verify a note as counterfeit. And usually the note would be counterfeit, but they wouldn't have a suspect...an unknown passer. We'd tell them to hold on to the counterfeit note and we'd swing by the casino in the morning on the way to the office and pick it up.

Donnie said he was sitting at his desk wrapping up a report before he headed home when the telephone rang. It was LVMPD calling to report a landlord had called and said one of his tenants was printing money in his rental house. Donnie needed me to come back to the office so we could go check it out. I told Donnie to call the Beaver and see if he could meet us at the office. Taking down a printing operation will probably take more than the two of us.

I gave the Redhead a kiss hello. "How was your day?" And I gave her a kiss good-bye. "I'll see you when I see you." She gave me the frown and asked when I would be back. "Some guy printing counterfeit." I said, "I'll be lucky if I'm home tomorrow night."

"Be careful," she said, and off I went.

I sat down in Donnie's office and he was wound up. The Beaver walked in and took a seat. He looked unhappy; he had that look on his face like he'd just started to pop the top on a cold beer when Donnie called him back to the office. Donnie said the LVMPD called the office at about five forty-five, just as he was getting ready to "roll" the office telephone over to our after-hours answering service. The PD said a Mr. Hargrove had reported his tenant was printing money in a rental house.

Donnie said he'd called Hargrove, who said he was renting his old family house to an older guy named Lucky Cargill. The rental house was located out in the desert on the northeast side of town, off of East Lake Mead Boulevard. Cargill had not paid rent for over six months and Hargrove had gone out to the property earlier that day to evict the tenant. When Cargill did not answer the door, Hargrove entered the house looking for him. What he found instead surprised him.

Inside the living room Hargrove saw a large printing press, cameras on tripods, and a big machine with a heat lamp in it. "I'm sure that's a plate burner," Donnie said. Hargrove also saw money printed on sheets of paper. Stacks and stacks of paper with printed money on them.

Donnie said he'd already spoke with T.J. over at the US Attorney's office and ran the scenario by him. T.J. told Donnie that we didn't need a search warrant for the house...if he hadn't paid rent in six months and the landlord was evicting him, he has no expectation to privacy in that residence.

It was getting close to six-thirty in the evening and on this hot summer night in Vegas we had about two or three hours of daylight. The Beaver and I took two cars and went out to find the residence and set up where we could see if Cargill was home yet or at least watch for him to return. Donnie went to meet Hargrove to get a written statement from him and a key to the house.

The Beaver and I stopped at strip mall near North Nellis Boulevard and East Lake Mead Boulevard, and he jumped into my Camaro. We drove east on Lake Mead Boulevard to find a couple of good spots to set up on the place. The house sat a couple of hundred yards south of Lake Mead Boulevard, in a large parcel of desert. It looked like a farmhouse that was at least fifty years old. While it had once sat all by itself way out in the middle of nowhere, now Las Vegas was slowly growing toward it. The house was surrounded by big cottonwood trees and bushes, it looked like a nice shady oasis in the desert.

The Beaver got out my binoculars and peered at the house. "I can't see shit," he told me. "It's impossible to see if anybody's home; too much vegetation." It was obvious we were going to need to do surveillance from two different angles, so we went back to get the Beaver's car; I set up west of the property on Lake Mead Boulevard and the Beaver went east a few blocks.

About an hour later Donnie hit us up on the radio and said to meet him to discuss Hargrove's statement and put together a plan. I told him to meet me back at the strip mall at Nellis and Lake Mead. The Beaver stayed put to watch the property.

Donnie said he got a good written statement from Hargrove; the living room had no furniture and it had been converted into a print shop. Hargrove said there was a table in the dining room with a paper cutter and scraps of paper all over the floor. And cats. Hargrove figured there were a dozen cats in the house and there was cat shit everywhere. "Oh boy," I said, "Fucking cat shit. This gonna be fun."

The Secret Service classifies all counterfeit notes by the Federal Reserve Bank, the faceplate, the check letter/quadrant number, and the back plate; these are those small letters and numbers you'll find on the notes. The serial numbers on an offset printed counterfeit are not relevant. A counterfeiter takes a photograph of a genuine Federal Reserve note, develops a negative from the film and burns that negative on to an offset plate. He has to make a minimum of three runs through the press: The first run to print black ink on the front of the note, the second, applies green ink to the back of the note and the third run to print green ink for the front serial number and Treasury seal.

Some counterfeiters used a fourth and fifth pass through the printer to simulate the red and blue fibers that were imbedded in genuine notes. Counterfeiters could easily change the serial number on a new run, by making a plate with just the serial number and Treasury Seal and changing to the serial number plate every so often. At least, that's the way it was done before digital printing, computers, and color copiers. In the old days, to print money you had to be skilled at the craft. Nowadays any knucklehead with a computer can try to counterfeit currency with the onset of this new technology.

In the 1990s we saw a dramatic increase in printer notes and Treasury responded by redesigning FRNs with hard to reproduce security features. But in the eighties when we ran across "printer" notes, we consider them junk and didn't put a lot of time into investigating them. We called them reproductions and most were impossible to pass on the public. That would change as the printing technology improved.

Every counterfeit note passed eventually ends up on the desk of a Secret Service agent, theoretically anyway, if the note finds its way to a bank, or merchant, or the Federal Reserve. New counterfeits are checked against known counterfeits for an internally assigned circular number. A new note required a forensic examination at our lab in Washington, DC, and new circular number would be assigned if it wasn't linked to a known counterfeit. Whenever we got a new note in our district we investigated the shit out of it, because that meant we had a new counterfeiter in operation. Donnie and I knew we hadn't had any new counterfeits lately, so that meant Cargill wasn't finished printing and he wasn't ready to get them into circulation. Looks like we got a lucky break on this case; we stopped it before it even got started.

In L.A. we might have conducted this investigation a little differently. We might have started a twenty-four-hour surveillance of Cargill to see who else was in on the printing. We might have tried to get a snitch into him and introduce an undercover agent. All the fun stuff. But this was Vegas; we had three agents and forty cases apiece. Donnie and I figured we'd just take this guy down and move on. The way to approach this situation: Walk up to the house, knock on the door and arrest the bastard.

I called the Beaver on the radio and told him to meet Donnie and me at the strip mall. The three of us jumped into Donnie's sedan. As we drove down the long gravel driveway, the house gradually exposed itself. We were approaching the house from the front and we could see a large backyard with no out buildings. There were no cars on the property. The driveway led to the back of the house, though the large trees. I jumped out of the car and walked around to cover the front of the house, in case Cargill was home and he bolted out the front door. The front of the house faced to the north, toward Lake Mead Boulevard. The grass was sparse and rusty beer cans littered the yard. The front door looked like it hadn't been opened since 1960. Donnie and the Beaver went to knock on the back door, adjacent to the gravel parking area at the end of the driveway. It was very obvious that the back door was used as the main entrance into the dwelling.

A few minutes later I could hear someone trying to open the front door and then a lot of pounding. *What the fuck? Is Cargill trying to escape?* Finally, I saw curtains part on the window to the side of the door. It was the Beaver and he was giving me the all-clear sign, which was him pantomiming the words "It's all clear."

I went around to the back and walked into the house. The stench made me want to gag. A couple of cats ran out the door as I entered the living room. It was dark and the one overhead light on the ceiling was blinking rapidly. There was an AB Dick 1200 offset printing press, the choice of all fine counterfeiters, sitting in the middle of the living room, along with two cameras, a camera tripod, negatives, printing plates, printed sheets of currency, and that big plate burner. The dining room table had printed sheets of counterfeit notes, some with three notes per page and some with four. *Might as well optimize your production, Lucky!* We saw one hundreds, fifties, twenties, and tens. Stacks of them in uncut sheets.

Donnie wanted to call the LVMPD evidence team to photograph the inside of the house. The Beaver and I exchanged glances. "Come on man," said the Beaver. "We've got cameras in our car."

"No. This is too big," said Donnie. The next thing I knew, Donnie was sitting in his G-ride on the LVMPD frequency of the radio and calling for help. I looked at the Beaver and just rolled my eyes. But Donnie is Donnie; he's the GS-13 here. The Beaver walked away and shook his head. Donnie always seemed to make a big deal out of everything.

As we waited for the PD evidence team, we did a search of the rooms. We found more stacks of counterfeit notes cut and bound with rubber bands in shoeboxes in a closet. The fifty-dollar counterfeits struck me as odd. The fifty was probably the least counterfeited note. A counterfeiter wants to make a note that is easily passed and the twenty was the number one counterfeited note, because they were plentiful and people used them all the time to make purchases at stores. Using a fifty-dollar bill might cause a store clerk to look at it a little closer; plus, fifties were consider bad luck in Las Vegas. "Never bet a fifty-dollar bill at a casino" was the Vegas lore. A sure way to jinx yourself and lose. Looked like Lucky Cargill jinxed himself all right, three Secret Service agents were standing in the middle of his printing operation.

By the time we finished searching the house and the evidence team got done lighting the inside up like a baseball stadium to photograph the plant, it was very late. Now what do we do? We'd just seized a big counterfeiting plant operation, but our printer was nowhere to be found. We decided we needed to set up a surveillance on the place and wait for him to come home. An LVMPD detective volunteered to stay and help us out. *Great! Now we have four guys, which is better than three.* We decided the best place to watch the property was right there in the backyard. Anybody approaching wouldn't see our cars until they were almost in the yard. The detective said he would set up on Lake Mead Boulevard to watch for cars turning into the driveway. We went to the strip mall and got the other two cars. We were in for a long night.

It was a clear and hot night in Vegas. From the backyard we good see the glow of Las Vegas, the Strip, and Glitter Gulch to the south. The moon was almost full and the darkened house took on a surreal look. I was expecting to see Lucky Cargill ride up in the moonlight on a horse with a pack mule behind him, an old gold miner returning to his claim and his paper gold.

It was about two in the morning and the Beaver was hungry. None of us had eaten since lunch and the Beaver volunteered to go get pizza. That's one of the things I loved about Las Vegas. It was a twenty-four-hour town; grocery stores, restaurants; shit, everything was open 24/7! Even the dry cleaners, for Pete's sake. Years later when the Redhead and I transferred out of Vegas back to the real world, we were shocked when we found out the local grocery store closed at ten in the evening.

The detective drove to the house to join us for dinner, a gourmet feast of four pizzas on the hood of Donnie's sedan. And the Beaver did the right thing by grabbing four cans of beer when he bought the pizzas. I devoured two or three slices and had just picked up a Bud and popped the top when the Beaver grabbed my arm and whispered, "There he is!"

I looked to the east and could faintly see a lone figure walking—actually, staggering—through the sagebrush toward the house. The Beaver took off running into the desert, I glanced at the can of beer and set it on the hood and followed behind him. Lucky Cargill was in custody and he was blind-stumbling drunk.

Donnie and I transported him to the office, while the detective and the Beaver started the long process of transporting the evidence. The LVMPD detective called for a uniformed cop to sit on the place until we could get a moving company over there to transport the large printing equipment to our evidence locker later that afternoon.

Donnie and I were interviewing Cargill in our suspect interview room and Lucky was cooperative with our investigation and answered all of our questions. I excused myself from the interview and started running him for wants, warrants, and criminal history.

I walked back into the interview room and tossed a rap sheet on the desk in front of Donnie. It turned out Lucky was on federal probation for counterfeiting US currency. A former Las Vegas agent, who was long transferred to Washington, DC, had arrested him for printing counterfeit currency almost six years ago. The rap sheet indicated a US district court judge had sentenced Lucky to ten years, suspended, to serve twelve months and five years probation. *Wow, he's got about three months left on his probation. With this arrest tonight his probation will be revoked and he'll do ten years, plus any sentence imposed on this new case will run consecutively. He could be looking at twenty years.*

I pulled the old case file and put it on my desk. Then I started writing an affidavit for the arrest warrant and Cargill's initial appearance before a US magistrate later that day.

An initial appearance before a US magistrate is a formal hearing where the defendant is formally advised of his rights before the court, advised of the charges against him, appointed an attorney, and if he can't afford one, have one assigned to his case…all that good legal stuff. A preliminary hearing date is set and the defendant is given a bond for his release.

Everything was going according to the book on Lucky's initial appearance. My AUSA was arguing for detention of the defendant as a flight risk and the assistant federal public defender was arguing for his release on bond. The typical courtroom dance. The AUSA and I knew Cargill was going to get detained without bail; he was on probation of counterfeiting currency and his US Probation officer was sitting in the front row of the courtroom. The charges he now faced were certain to get his probation revoked. And then one of the most unusual things I've ever heard a probation officer say happened.

The judge was considering detaining Cargill, but the public defender was talking nonstop about how Cargill was not a flight risk, he'd always made all his court appearances on the previous case that led to his probation, and suddenly the judge was wavering; I could feel it. The judge looked at the Probation officer and asked if she was going to revoke his probation.

"No," she said and I almost fell out of my chair. *Are you kidding me?* She continued saying the current charges were based on a probable cause affidavit and she wouldn't consider a revocation hearing until Cargill was indicted by a grand jury. The AUSA leaped right in with some good arguments about how that was then and this is now, and he was facing significant jail time on the revocation and significant jail time on these charges. He must be detained.

But the judge wasn't buying it. The defendant had a record of making his court appearances and he couldn't speculate on future events; Cargill was released on his own recognizance. That meant he did not have to place a monetary bond with the court; his word was his bond and he promised to come back to court for his next appearance. I was shocked. *Okay, grant him bond if you want, but at least make him come up with five thousand dollars to secure his release, please!*

Lucky Cargill walked out of that courtroom a free man. And he knew he would be indicted and he knew he was going to prison for violating the conditions of his probation. Lucky Cargill knew he would be found guilty on my new charges of counterfeiting US currency and he would be sentenced to more prison time for these charges, and the sentences would more than like run consecutively. He was looking at some serious federal time. So he did what any crook with a few brains would do. He vanished into thin air and it would be a long, long time before he surfaced.

I spent a lot of time in the next few years looking for him. The US Marshals issued wanted posters, I requested that agents interview his known family members in Montana, I got subpoenas for telephone records...all that stuff. I even tried to talk headquarters in putting his story on a new television series that was very popular in the late eighties—*America's Most Wanted.* But the Secret Service had not been featured on the television show yet and headquarters turned down my request. The Counterfeit Division agent told me they were looking to get a Secret Service fugitive case to submit to the producers of the show, but they felt the Cargill case lacked enough pizzazz. I couldn't have disagreed more.

So, Lucky faded away into the desert. He obviously changed his habits and quit counterfeiting money and he was never arrested again for committing any crime. I did indict him, for so many counts of manufacturing and possession of counterfeit currency that my grand jury testimony took half the day. And the Probation officer finally revoked his probation…two warrants out there in, what we would call today, cyberspace. But Lucky never had another encounter with a police officer until the winter of the year 2000, about twelve years later.

Lucky Cargill was in Reno, Nevada. He was one of those homeless guys you see on the freeway off-ramp with a cup and a sign. Late one winter night the Reno Police Department responded to a call about an unresponsive man in a city park. Lucky Cargill was transported to the local hospital and was diagnosed with dementia and kidney failure. He passed away shortly thereafter.

I often thought about Lucky over the years and wondered, where did he go and what did he do? Donnie used to goad the shit out of me about him…every once in a while, I would get a letter in the mail or a telephone call. It was always Donnie, with a crayon written note or in a gravely voice on the phone and the message was always the same, "You'll never catch me, copper!"

Lucky was about fifty-five years old on that moonlit summer night when he walked through the desert toward his house. As we wrapped up our interview of Lucky and prepared to take him to the Clark County Jail, I asked him why he came back to the house. I mean, he knew we were there searching the place. He knew he was on probation for counterfeiting US currency. He knew he'd be going to jail. He could have just disappeared right then and there. "Why come back to the house and face immediate arrest Lucky?"

"I was sitting in a bar up on Lake Mead Boulevard," he said to me, "And could see all the commotion down there about midnight. The inside of the house was lit up like Christmas."

I looked at Lucky and I could see his pale blue eyes tearing up. "Why'd you come home Lucky?" I repeated.

Lucky paused for a few seconds with his head down and his elbows on the arms of the chair, his hands were clasps on his lap. He rubbed his eyes. A teardrop fell on his pant leg. "I..." he was struggling for the words. "I, well...I had to feed my cats."

Chapter 6

Joe the Cubs Fan

Every now and then—like most Fridays after work—the three of us would stop by a tucked away bar/restaurant across the street from the federal building in Las Vegas. It was the destination of choice for most federal law enforcement agents, probation officers, AUSAs and the occasional assistant federal public defender. It was an Irish pub-style joint and it was a great place to enjoy a cocktail without worrying you'd run into some low-life you'd once arrested.

The Beaver and I were having a beer at the pub one Friday evening with a couple of buddies from ATF, when one of the ATF agent's beeper went off and he excused himself to find the pay phone. After the agent made his way back to our table, he leaned in to my ear and asked if I was interested in talking to an informant about a guy with some counterfeit. He said he was working a reliable informant on some illegal gun cases and his guy just called. "You available tomorrow afternoon to meet this guy?" *Me? Available tomorrow? Saturday? You bet I am!*

This informant was a professional. And by that I mean he was in it for the money. The Secret Service didn't have a lot of money to throw around at snitches; most of our informants were arrestees that were working "off the beef," arrestees who agreed to provide information to us against the other members of the conspiracy, in exchange for leniency from the US Attorney. Working with a professional informant was always a little dicey for us... we couldn't pay these guys much and there's no telling what he expected. The DEA was known for paying big money to informants for drug seizures, but you have to remember we were investigating counterfeit currency; and counterfeit money is worthless, it has no value. So seizing a million dollars of worthless counterfeit was not the same as seizing a million dollars worth of cocaine. I had to be careful and up front with this guy.

It turned out the professional didn't really care. He had just run into a guy named Joe Mullane at a local bar and Joe was looking for a guy to bankroll a printing operation and he picked the wrong guy to confide his plans in. The ATF informant had never seen this guy before and he could give a shit about him and his counterfeit operation. The informant said he would gladly make an introduction of my guy to Joe for one hundred dollars and then he wanted out of the picture.

The ATF informant got in touch with Joe and told him he knew a guy that might have some money to invest, "Give him a call, he owns a bar in Henderson and he's always looking to make a buck. His name is Mike." The snitch gave Joe our undercover telephone number and I paid him one hundred dollars. Then we waited for Joe to call.

I was sitting in the Beaver's office and we were discussing an antelope hunt in east central Nevada, up near Ely. The Beaver had a permit for one antelope on a rare summer deprivation hunt on a rancher's property. It seemed the rancher's alfalfa fields were being destroyed by a small herd of antelopes and the State didn't take kindly to ranchers being annoyed by antelope. The Nevada Department of Wildlife put eleven permits out for a lottery draw. The Beaver drew one and I didn't, but I was going with him to keep him out of trouble. We were supposed to leave the next weekend on Sunday, and hunt Monday, Tuesday and Wednesday.

We heard the undercover telephone ringing down the hall and dashed to the room. I closed the door just as the Beaver pushed the record button and said hello. It was Joe. He said he understood "Mike" was a businessman and he had a business proposal. He wanted to meet with "Mike" at the sports book bar at the Desert Inn. Joe said he would be sitting at the bar wearing a Cubs ball cap. He said he had some samples of his proposition to show "Mike."

One thing we didn't want Joe to do was control the investigation. We didn't have time to get our act together to run over to the Desert Inn, so "Mike" said he was working but he could meet him around six o'clock that evening at the parking lot of the First Interstate Bank Building on Paradise Road. "Mike" said he was driving a white IROC-Z Camaro and he'd park on the south side of he lot. "And wear your Cubs cap," added the Beaver as he winked at me.

Secret Service agents are privileged to drive government cars, with home to work authority and we all knew the cars weren't ours, but a guy does get attached to his G-ride. I've seen some crazy arguments and backstabbing over the years when new G-rides arrive at an office. Donnie was always trying to get my Camaro back—it had once been assigned to him. I looked at the Beaver and reminded him we had an undercover car specifically for these types of meets. The Beaver reminded me that he was a businessman in this undercover assignment and he couldn't drive that piece-of-shit sedan that screamed "Law Enforcement officer" to a meet.

About an hour before the meet, Donnie went over to a three-story parking garage that overlooked the south side of the meet site and picked a nice spot in the shade to see if Mullane had any countersurveillance planned.

The boss parked across the street in the Citibank branch lot, and I took the surveillance van and parked on the south side of the First Interstate Bank building, nose in with the rear, facing south. The Beaver was supposed to pull in opposite my location and park facing south. At six o'clock on a weekday, the parking lot would be empty, with plenty of room for us to maneuver.

The Beaver got all wired up and drove to the meet site. As he drove toward our positions he was talking to me through the UHF transmitter and it was loud and clear. He pulled into the lot at about five minutes to six; he got out of the car and sat on the hood of my Camaro. All 280 pounds of him. I could see the hood bending under is butt. *If you put a permanent dent in the hood of my Camaro, you can eat cheeseburgers with Donnie.* Joe pulled in at a few minutes after six.

Joe was driving a beat-up old Datsun two-door with the right rear taillight smashed in and he had a woman with him. The Datsun coupe was a sun-faded blue that looked almost white. A few coats of wax and some shade would've done that Datsun some good when it was still shiny blue. The Vegas sun is brutal on car finishes and you could tell Joe didn't take care of it. The woman looked to be about eighteen to twenty years old. I had a great view out the back windows of the van; the Beaver was just across the parking lot, directly opposite the surveillance van. The parking lot was completely empty, just has we had guessed it would be. Bankers... what a great job; you get to go home Monday through Friday after an eight-hour day and you don't work weekends.

Joe parked right next to the surveillance van. With the height advantage, I could peer out the side windows on our surveillance van directly inside the Datsun at the girl sitting in the passenger's side. She sat there looking bored as Joe met with the Beaver over by my Camaro.

Joe said he worked at a Las Vegas print shop and he was an experienced printer. He said he was going to print counterfeit money at the print shop where he worked, after everybody else had left for the day. Joe looked to be in his early twenties, not much older than "Trixie" sitting in the Datsun. *Years of experience. I'm sure you do. And a Cubs fan to boot.* Joe said he needed three hundred dollars to buy some high-quality paper in order for the bills to be passable. Joe told "Mike" he was going to print $100,000 in twenties.

The Beaver looked at Joe and asked, "How the hell do you print counterfeit money?" Joe proceeded to give "Mike" a quick lesson on the art of counterfeiting; and he was right on target with his description. The Beaver played dumb and wanted to know how anybody could pass that stuff, and said, "Does it look that real?"

"I've got a sample with me," Joe told the Beaver, "one that I printed before I left Chicago."

Joe walked over toward the passenger's side of the Datsun. His back was blocking my view from the side window of the surveillance van. I could tell he was talking to the girl. I was worried she might be giving him a gun, so I narrated the movements of Joe for Donnie and the boss, "S-one said he had a sample in his car. He's walking to his vehicle." I said, "Stand by." But when Joe turned to go back to Beaver, I could plainly see his hands and all he had was one bill. I glanced over and saw Trixie zipping her purse. "S-two handed him one note. S-one walking over to our guy, all clear. Stand by."

Joe handed the Beaver a counterfeit five-dollar bill. "Looks pretty good, are you sure this is counterfeit?"

"Oh, yeah," Joe bragged, "I'm really good. And with the high-quality paper they are completely undetectable! I can print anything." I love a crook that brags, especially when it's on tape.

The Beaver wanted to know what was in it for him, if he were to provide the three hundred dollars for the paper.

Joe said he would print "Mike" one hundred thousand dollars' worth of counterfeit twenties for ten thousand real cash. "You could sell those for twenty-five to thirty cents on the dollar, easy," said Joe. "You could triple your ten-thousand-dollar investment."

"Mike" said that was a pretty good return on his money, but he wanted to know where the print shop was located. "No offense, Joe," said the Beaver, "but I just met ya and this seems too good to be true. Are you a cop?"

"No, no, no," said Joe, "I just need to make a little cash. I just need an investor. My cash flow is a little low right now. The print shop is over on Highland and I can take you by there and show you. I'm legit. We can go right now," said Joe. He was obviously anxious to seal this deal.

The Beaver told Joe that he had to get going; he had things to do tonight, but he'd meet him tomorrow night at around nine at the print shop and give him the three hundred dollars. The Beaver added, "Can I keep this five?"

"Sure," said Joe. "The shop is just north of Spring Mountain Road, across from Walt's Bar."

The boss and Donnie followed Joe as he drove south on Paradise Road. The Beaver watched Joe exit the parking lot, got in my Camaro, and drove north on Paradise Road. I stayed put in the van until Donnie called me on the radio to report Joe was eastbound on Tropicana and clear of the area.

I met the Beaver in the parking lot at our office and we walked inside to wait for Donnie and the boss to return. I ran the license plate on the Datsun and it came back to a Michelle Edison, on Sierra Vista, Las Vegas. When Donnie and the boss walked in, they said Joe and the girl drove to an apartment complex on Sierra Vista, got out, and walked into one of the units on the main floor of the building.

The four of us sat in the boss's office and listened to the tape recording of the meeting. The Beaver said, "I don't know about this guy, he's awful anxious and fidgety. He's a drug addict no doubt."

The boss said, "We have to be careful with this one guys, this smells like a setup."

At nine o'clock the next night, Donnie, the boss, and I set up a surveillance to cover the Beaver at the print shop. Beaver waited out by my Camaro and Joe walked outside to meet him. "Come on in," he said to the Beaver. "I'll give you a tour."

"Hey listen," said the Beaver, "Something came up and I can't stay long. But run this by me again would you. If I pay you ten thousand dollars, you'll print and sell me one hundred thousand dollars in counterfeit twenty-dollar bills? And I have to buy this paper you need?"

"Oh yeah, absolutely. Good, high-quality funny money!"

"Well, as a businessman, it seems I'm taking all the risk. How do I know you won't just take my money and run?"

"Normally I don't operate like this," said Joe, "But I just started this job and haven't got my first paycheck yet. I wouldn't fuck ya. I swear I wouldn't."

The Beaver handed Joe three crisp one-hundred-dollar bills and said, "Here is three hundred dollars. I want you to call me second you get the paper. And if I don't answer, leave me a voice mail. Then call me when you're ready to start printing."

"Oh yeah, thanks Mike. I will, I will. We're partners now."

* * *

On Sunday morning the Beaver and I took off for Ely. His pickup was crammed full of our camping gear and coolers, some for beer and some for antelope. We figured we would get up there early and do what we do best, knock on the door of the rancher's house.

introduce our selves, and say hello. Might as well make a new best friend, especially if he had lots of acreage for hunting. You never know; fall was around the corner and he might have mule deer, elk, turkey, pheasants, and quail. This place could be our hunting heaven. We surmised he was a Mormon, as a lot of folk in the rural areas out west are. The Beaver, being a Catholic from Utah, told me not to worry. A lot of his pals in the PD back in Salt Lake City were Mormons and he said he knew the secret handshake.

The rancher's name was Ethan and he was a good guy, friendly as hell, as most folks who live in the middle of nowhere are. Ethan invited us to camp on his ranch and showed us a good spot down by a spring, right in the center of his alfalfa fields. Great spot; we could wake up and wait for the antelope to come to us. Sunday evening he stopped by and had a beer with us. *He must be a Jack Mormon.*

Monday morning we were up early and I was thinking a good hot cup of coffee was just what we needed to take the chill off. There was a frost on the ground and I was shivering, it had been close to one hundred degrees Sunday afternoon and now I was freezing. It was a new moon and it was darker than shit. I stared at the eastern horizon as it was just starting to glow pink. *Come on sun...get up!* I started to build a fire for the coffee pot, when the Beaver said, "Cover your ears!"

There was an antelope forty feet in front of us, I could just barely make out his shape in the darkness, the Beaver shot, and I was standing right next to him. *Jesus fucking Christ!* I didn't get my hands up to my ears and now they were ringing to beat the band. I could barely see the outline of the antelope as he ran away. "You asshole!" I said, "How could you miss that shot, Beaver?"

"Ethan said there were about thirty of 'em in here," said the Beaver. "I'll have plenty more chances." It took a couple of hours before my hearing returned too normal.

We didn't see another antelope until Wednesday. As Monday and Tuesday progressed, I was counting the shots in the distance. The other hunters, the ones that didn't get the prime camping spot on Ethan's property, were killing antelope left and right. By Wednesday morning, we heard shot number ten ring out. Now it looked like "Mr. Number Eleven" was the last hunter standing. Ethan stopped by our camp about lunchtime to see how we doing. It wasn't going too good, we had not seen an antelope since Monday morning. "Go to the far south end of the ranch," he said, "And glass up alongside the hillside to the west. During the hot part of the day, you'll see their horns poking up over the sagebrush as they try to cool down in shade." And believe me, that desert was hot that day.

We took off in the Beaver's pickup and drove the three miles down a dirt road that bisected the ranch. We spent a good two hours glassing the hillside and didn't see shit. Suddenly, I saw a huge plume of dust to the north. *What the heck?* Somebody was driving very fast in our direction. I put the binoculars up to my eyes and saw it was Ethan on his tractor heading toward us and he had that tractor at full speed. I immediately thought something was wrong—maybe there was an accident? We got in the truck and headed north to intercept Ethan to see how we could help.

Ethan screeched to a halt in front of us and dust went flying like crazy. He looked at the Beaver, "You want an antelope? There's a big buck in my alfalfa field and he ain't scared of my tractor, so jump on." The Beaver slung the rifle on his shoulder, stood on the back of the tractor holding on the back of the seat and off they went back north. I waited a few minutes to let the dust settle and followed in the truck.

When I got back up near the alfalfa field, I grabbed the binoculars to get a good look. The Beaver was covered in light brown dust...I mean covered. He was standing next to that dark red tractor, not thirty yards from a very large antelope. The antelope was grazing on the alfalfa, not even paying any attention to Ethan, the Beaver or the tractor. The Beaver wiped dirt and sweat from his eyes and worked the bolt on the rifle. He was using the tractor for cover and he tried to use the hood of that Massey Ferguson as a brace, but the hood was hot and he jerked his arm off real quick and let out a yelp. Mr. Antelope could have cared less. The Beaver took a deep breath and assumed a nice standing position with the rifle at his shoulder. He squeezed the trigger and the antelope dropped like a dishtowel on the kitchen floor. I could see Ethan sitting on the tractor laughing his ass off.

I walked across the field to see the kill. The Beaver was caked with dust and he was spitting mud, but he finally got an antelope.

* * *

Thursday morning I went in the office early and started checking the incoming message traffic to the office, to see what was happening Service wide while I'd been on leave. The Riverside Resident Agency had sent out a new counterfeit note report to our Counterfeit Division in DC. A new counterfeit twenty had been passed at a fast food place near Ontario, California. The local PD had responded and interviewed the passer. His name was Douglas Henry and he was from Las Vegas. The Ontario PD arrested Henry for forgery and he was released on bond.

A new counterfeit note...that was interesting. Somebody had a printing operation going and it might just be in Las Vegas. No one else had come in to the office yet, so I locked the door and set the burglar alarm. I jumped into my IROC-Z and drove to the Henry address to snoop around a little. Maybe Joe had printed that counterfeit and maybe he didn't. You just never knew until you start investigating.

The address listed for Henry was east of the airport off of Hacienda and Pecos Road, a residential area with middle class homes. No cars were in the driveway and no cars were parked in front of the house on the street. I drove to Spring Mountain and made a drive-by of Joe's print shop on Highland to get some plates from cars in their parking lot. I wanted to see if any one working at the print shop was named Henry or had cars registered to Henry's address. I came up empty. It was about nine in the morning after I finished running the plates with LVMPD and started to head back to the office. I decided to do one more drive-by at the Henry residence to see if any cars had shown up.

There still were no vehicles at the house and the scene hadn't changed much since my first visit at around seven that morning, except for a young guy, maybe late teens early twenties mowing the front yard. *What the hell, I'll stop by and introduce myself.* As we stood in the front yard under the shade of an old mesquite tree, the kid said his name was Douglas Henry Junior and he was nineteen. He said his dad was at work and there was no mom.

I asked him about the counterfeit note and I could tell he suddenly became extremely nervous. I decided to play nice guy and explained Title 18 United States Code Section 471, and the penalties for printing counterfeit currency. I told him people who cooperate with an investigation have a very good chance, especially if they have no criminal record, of getting the US Attorney to help them out. Not everybody goes to jail. We went into the house and sat in the living room. It was time to get serious…I advised Henry of his Miranda rights and he started talking.

"I printed the counterfeit," he told me.

"Where?" I asked.

"In our garage," he said.

"Can I see?"

We walked back outside and he opened the garage. I stood at the opening of the garage and peered in at a complete counterfeiting operation; an AB Dick 1200 offset printing press, cameras, and a huge plate maker. Junior said the printing equipment belonged to his father, Douglas Sr. He told me his dad was printing flyers for local businesses trying to make a little extra money for the family. Dad was hoping to turn the garage print shop into a full—time small business. Junior said he counterfeited one twenty-dollar bill just for fun, to see if he could do it. I had trouble believing this nineteen-year-old kid had counterfeited one note for fun or that he'd done this project by himself with no help from Pops.

I just seized a counterfeit plant! I got on the Motorola radio and called the office. Donnie answered up. "Hey, can you and the Beaver come over here and help me out? I got a counterfeit plant in this guy's garage."

"You did what?" Donnie laughed. He was in total disbelief.

"Just hustle over here," I said. "I need some help."

Junior was very cooperative and he seemed relieved to be getting all of this off his chest. We did a consent search of the house and didn't find any counterfeit. No plates, no negatives. Nothing. Not even paper scraps in the trash. Maybe he was telling the truth; maybe he did only print one note for fun. But my gut told me probably not. Donnie called the boss at the office and asked him to come to the house to help out. When the boss arrived he looked at me and asked, "What case is this? Mullane? I didn't know you guys were working on another counterfeit plant case."

"It's kind of a new one," I said, "I'll explain later." The Beaver and I loaded Junior in his G-ride and I left the keys to my IROC-Z with Donnie. "I want those back, big guy." I said to Donnie.

He laughed and said, "Don't worry, I don't want your fucking G-ride and don't worry about all this heavy evidence in the garage. I'll take care of it for you."

This was going to be a long day. And we still had to finish up with Joe.

Chapter 7

100 Percent Cotton Paper

When we got to the office, Junior held fast to his story of "I only printed one counterfeit twenty" and I just wasn't buying it. His explanation of things didn't make sense. A good lie requires plausibility; it has got to be possible and more importantly, it has to make common sense. We could not believe that this nineteen-year-old kid had printed the counterfeit twenty with no help from the old man and that he had only printed one.

"So, where is Senior?" I asked him. "What's he do for a living? Where does he work?"

"He works at a lithograph shop in Henderson," said Junior. *A lithograph shop!* So the old man is a printer by trade and not just "trying" to start a small business in his garage to make a few extra bucks for the family. It was time to interview Senior.

I stopped by the boss's office to advise him Junior was in the lockup and he said, "Close the door." I figured I was in for an ass chewing for conducting a suspect interview without backup. "I thought you knew better than that," he said.

"I'm sorry boss," I said, "I wasn't sure who the kid was and before I knew it he was confessing to counterfeiting."

"Yeah, well don't you ever do that again," he scolded, then he smiled, "But...good job, a counterfeiting plant out of thin air!"

Beaver and I left Junior secured in our lockup and drove to the address for Senior's employer. We walked into the lithograph shop and identified ourselves to the owner as US Secret Service agents and he led us into his small office and closed the door. I told him I would like to speak with Douglas Henry. "Is he in trouble? He's one of my longest tenured employees."

"No," I said, "I just need to asked him a couple of questions."

The owner picked up his phone, dialed four numbers, and said, "Doug, can you come to my office?"

A few minutes later, the door opened, "Are you Douglas Henry, Senior?" I asked.

"Yes," he replied.

I looked at the owner and then said to Senior, "Let's step outside, this won't take long."

The Beaver and I escorted Senior out of the front door to the sidewalk. The first thing out of his mouth was, "Can we talk later this evening?" He didn't ask who we were or why we were interrupting his workday.

I showed him my credentials and said, "Listen, Pop, Junior is sitting in my interview room right now and he's looking at federal time. Perhaps you should take the day off and come with us."

The ride in the Beavers G-ride back to our office was a quiet one. I was a little surprised he didn't ask me any questions. He and I sat in the backseat and he stared out the passenger side window the whole way downtown. We brought Senior into my office and told him he was not under arrest and he was free to terminate the interview and walk out at any time. "I need to get to the bottom of this," I told him. "I need the truth about this counterfeiting operation and I need your help to do that." Senior was evasive and claimed he didn't know anything. Right away the Beaver and I knew he was hiding something. *Of course, he helped the kid print the counterfeit twenty; he was a printer, for Christ's sake!*

"If you cooperate with this investigation," I told him, "I will advise the US Attorney. You have no criminal history...only good things can happen if you cooperate and only bad things can happen if you don't. The kid is looking at twenty years for counterfeiting; do you really want that for your son?"

At that point, Senior started to break...but he continued to minimize his participation. He said he knew the kid was trying to counterfeit money. He figured he was just playing around, getting used to the process, after all the process is the same no matter what you are trying to reproduce with your printer. He didn't think the kid was serious about counterfeiting money and he never thought the kid would be stupid enough to try and pass a counterfeit note.

"Look," I said, "I know you helped him. I know you did." I leaned forward in my chair and got very close to his face. In a low, serious voice I said, "Listen very carefully to me." I paused for a second and then continued, "We found a small stack of twenties in the garage and if your fingerprints are on any of those, I will charge you and you can go to prison with him. Maybe the judge will order the Bureau of Prisons to place you guys in the same cell, so you can be together...father and son."

He hung his head. Now, we were starting to get somewhere. at any minute, he would crack.

"I thought we buried it all!" he said. He looked up at me and continued, "I knew the kid was counterfeiting money in the garage. I swear, I just thought he was playing around. When I found out I was shocked, and when the kid got arrested in Ontario for passing one, I knew it was time to get rid of all money he'd printed and all the evidence." Senior continued, "We took all the counterfeit money, all the negatives and all the plates out in the desert south of Henderson, dug a hole, and burned it all. Then we filled the hole in with dirt."

We went back in to the interview room to see Junior. "I know you burned and buried the evidence and I know you printed more than one twenty. It's time to tell the truth." I told Junior, "It's over. Now help me wrap this case up. Take me out to the desert and show me the hole."

By now it was lunchtime and the Beaver wanted a cheeseburger, but lunch would have to wait. I called T.J. at the US Attorney's office. "Take them to find the evidence." he said. "And then book them in the Clark County Jail. They'll see the magistrate tomorrow afternoon."

Once a federal arrest is made, an agent has to get the defendant before the "nearest" US magistrate as soon as possible: you can't just drive them around or have them sit in a holding cell for a few days. I'd placed Junior in custody at about nine thirty that morning. so normally he'd make his appearance before the magistrate that afternoon. But due to the fact the defendants were cooperating with the investigation, T.J. would be able to articulate the delay to the US magistrate judge.

We drove out into the desert on a dirt road south of Henderson. Junior and Senior were having trouble remembering the exact spot. "Come on, guys!" I said, "Think! Because we are staying out here until we find this shit." *Besides, the Bearer is hungry*. Finally we rounded a bend and came to an area at the base of a large hillside. Lots of trash littered the ground and you could tell people used the hillside for a target range.

"Stop here," Senior said.

We walked out toward the hill and kicked around a little. The kid found some charcoal markings and said, "Here, right here is where we burned it. This is the hole."

I opened the trunk and handed Dad a shovel. "Start digging."

I looked at the Beaver and smiled, "What do you think the New York FO Counterfeit Squad is doing today?"

I don't know," said the Beaver, "but you can bet they aren't digging up counterfeit plates out in the middle of the desert."

We ended up recovering several partially burned counterfeit twenties, one good unburned negative, and one metal plate that was still readable. There were enough whole notes to charge Junior with manufacturing and possessing $22,000 in counterfeit.

My problem was Senior. I just couldn't prove he was in on the manufacturing of the notes, but I could prove, through his confession, that he aided and abetted with the destruction of evidence; Title 18 United States Code Section 3, Accessory after the Fact: "Whoever, knowing that an offense against the United States has been committed, receives, relieves, comforts or assists the offender in order to hinder or prevent his apprehension, trial or punishment, is an accessory after the fact." That was the first and only time I used that statute…

They both ended up pleading guilty and the old man stuck to his story all the way through sentencing. And nobody believed him, including the US district court judge who sentenced him to prison for four years, plus three years' probation and 250 hours' community service. Junior lucked out and got three years' probation.

Community service—I always wondered what that entailed—picking up litter on Highway 95? Washing the windows at the Senior Center? One day a few years later I was at the Las Vegas airport catching a flight and guess who was running the big vacuum cleaner on the carpets at McCarran International? Douglas Henry, Senior. He must have got out early for good behavior.

* * *

Joe finally called "Mike" and told him he had the paper and he was going to start printing the counterfeit that night after the print shop closed. I just started putting an operations plan together for the surveillance of Joe, and the undercover telephone rang again.

It was Joe calling "Mike" again. Joe said he needed to meet with "Mike" right away and it was extremely urgent. Joe said a problem had come up with the printing and Joe wanted "Mike" to come by his apartment of Sierra Vista. Now we knew this was a setup. Joe was likely not even going to print counterfeit, so the Beaver put on the UHF transmitter and we sent the surveillance team to Sierra Vista. Our intent was to arrest Joe for conspiracy to manufacture counterfeit currency and possession of counterfeit (the counterfeit five-dollar bill he had given "Mike" at their first meet). T.J. told us to arrest the girl too, as part of the conspiracy.

The Beaver pulled into the apartment complex, got out of my Camaro, and leaned against the driver's side door. After a few minutes Joe came out of the building. He walked over to the Beaver and said there were some problems at the print shop and he needed two thousand dollars to buy more supplies. The Beaver gave the arrest signal and four federal agents materialized out of what I'm sure Joe thought was thin air. He was in custody and just as we were putting him in the back of Donnie's sedan, the girl, Michelle, drove into the parking lot, bad timing on her part, and good timing for us. We placed her under arrest.

Back at the office Donnie and I interviewed Joe and he came around real quick once we introduced the Beaver to him. He admitted he was planning to rob "Mike" of the two thousand dollars. He said originally he planned to print the counterfeit, but he changed his mind after he'd been fired from the print shop within minutes of calling "Mike" to the say he was ready to start printing that night. Michelle had a slightly different story: she told us his operation was a setup from the get-go. After he met "Mike" he figured the guy had money—he was the owner of a bar—so Joe told her he was only going to print the backs of counterfeit twenties, show them to "Mike," and steal his ten thousand dollars.

Crooks…you can't trust them.

We obtained and executed a search warrant for their small apartment on Sierra Vista. We didn't find any counterfeit or evidence of counterfeiting; but there was plenty of marijuana and cocaine.

Joe and Michelle pleaded guilty in US district court. Joe got six months in prison and five years' probation. Michelle got five years' probation.

Over the next five years both would have their probation revoked for using drugs, and the US district court judge would sentence them to a treatment facility, followed by more probation. This pattern repeated itself three or four times—they just couldn't stay off the cocaine.

Eventually, the judge had enough. He had been more than lenient with them and had given them numerous opportunities to clean up and live right. Michelle ended up doing nine months in a federal prison. Joe did another six months.

* * *

The 1988 presidential campaign was coming up, and headquarters was beginning to assign field agents to the candidates. Vice President George H. W. Bush was running for the Republican nomination, and he already had a permanent detail, but the field for the Democrats was wide-open and it seemed like dozens of them were running. Senator Joe Biden from Delaware, Senator Paul Simon from Illinois, Governor Michael Dukakis from Massachusetts, former governor Bruce Babbitt from Arizona, Senator Al Gore from Tennessee, former senator Gary Hart from Colorado, Representative Dick Gephardt from Missouri, and the Reverend Jesse Jackson were the main candidates, and each had a detail assigned to him at some point during the state primaries.

I was assigned to the protection detail for Senator Paul Simon and I left Las Vegas on a sunny January day headed for cold, gray Iowa. We bounced all over the state of Iowa; I mean from one end to the other. Senator Simon's campaign was on a shoestring budget, and most of this bouncing required us to drive from one campaign stump to the next. Occasionally, he would board his campaign plane; for example, a trip to New Hampshire in a small four-seat prop aircraft. We would load the senator and his staff on board that prop plane, watch him take off, then jump in our leased business jet, pass him mid-flight, and be there to pick up him up when he landed.

In those days, the candidate's protection details were comprised of agents from field offices around the nation. We spent twenty-one days on the detail and then twenty-one days back at our duty station. Each shift worked one week on day shift, followed by a week on midnights and finally a week on afternoon shift. With all the traveling from one city to another it was impossible to work an eight-hour day. We ended up working sixteen-hour days with the senator; day shift would work eight in the morning until midnight, while the afternoon shift would spend the day traveling to the next city where the senator was planning to spend the night, so that they would be ready to report for duty at eight the next morning. The midnight shift worked from midnight to 8 a.m. at the hotel where the senator was sleeping. Midnights were brutal: work all night, pile into rental cars, and drive to the next city and the next hotel, try to sleep a few hours, and be ready to go to work at midnight.

In 1988, the campaign really put a strain on the manpower of the Secret Service. Even a big field office like L.A. was short of agents to work our criminal investigations. I was back in Vegas for my twenty-one days in the field, when the boss told me L.A. needed some help on a counterfeit case. A twenty-four-hour surveillance of a printing operation. I was finally going to work a counterfeit case in L.A.!

The LAFO Counterfeit Squad got a call from a major paper supply house. In order to print descent and passable counterfeit notes, a bad guy needs good paper. Genuine notes are printed on 100 percent cotton paper. That's why that ten-dollar bill you left in your pants pocket that went through the washer and dryer was still pliable and wasn't completely destroyed; because the paper that genuine note was printed on is just like the blue jeans of whose pocket it was in during the wash cycle...100 percent cotton.

100 percent cotton paper is expensive and it is a bit unusual for a print shop to order up a large quantity because it was typically only used for the finest, most expensive printing jobs. Agents would conduct "supply house canvasses" of the larger paper distributors, educating them on what to look for if an individual wanted to buy 100 percent cotton fiber printing paper. We asked them to call the Secret Service if they received a suspicious order for this expensive paper.

The LAFO got a "paper squeal" from a distributor. Audie Stanton pulled up to a paper distributor in an old green Ford station wagon, placed an order and paid a cash deposit for reams of 100 percent cotton fiber paper. The manager thought this was an odd request for a guy driving an old station wagon: legitimate print shops usually arrived in a van or small truck, so he called the LAFO. Mr. Stanton was picking up his order tomorrow morning and the LAFO told him to complete the sale. Then they set up an operations plan to put a twenty-four-hour surveillance on Stanton to see what he was up to.

I had arrived in L.A. the night before and reported into the ATSAIC of the Counterfeit Squad early that morning. Due to campaign staffing we only had eleven agents to work the surveillance; five two-man G-rides and one poor soul inside the surveillance van. Luckily, that wasn't me.

We started the surveillance at the paper distributor and Audie Stanton showed up when they opened at nine in the morning. We watched him load that green Ford station wagon with so many reams of paper, the rear end was riding low. Looked like Audie needed some new shocks on that Ford. We followed him to his print shop in South Central L.A. and watched him unload it all and take it in the back door of the printing business.

The L.A. Counterfeit Squad was very familiar with Audie. He'd been arrested five or six times by the LAFO for counterfeiting. And it looked like he was up to it again. Audie had a print shop on Crenshaw Boulevard in South Central L.A. near the intersection of Florence and Crenshaw—an intersection that would become very famous during the Rodney King riots a few years later.

We watched him lock up and leave that evening; we followed him home and put him to bed. Once he left we had some of the guys check the trash Dumpster in the back of the print shop, hoping to find some evidence of counterfeiting, but we came up empty.

This routine went on for a few days, and it wasn't long before every swinging dick in South Central L.A. knew the cops were hanging out in the neighborhood. Those folks were pretty attuned to spotting white guys sitting in cars day-in and day-out in one general area around Crenshaw and Florence. Everybody except Audie...he didn't have a clue. We had the surveillance van parked across the street and down about a half of a block from Audie's print shop with a great view of the front door. Sitting in that surveillance van for twelve hours or more was uncomfortable, to say the least. Thank God I didn't get that assignment.

Some of the citizens of South Central L.A. were not shy about walking right up to our cars and asking us who we were looking for. The crack cocaine epidemic was at its peak back in 1988 and they all figured we were LAPD or the DEA waiting to bust a drug dealer. We had to wrap this investigation up real soon or risk Audie finally figuring out he was our target.

We were stuck and getting nowhere. We had no snitch on this case. We had no undercover agent in on this one. We were flying blind and needed a break to develop probable cause for an arrest. It didn't help that President Reagan was scheduled to go to his ranch in Santa Barbara for a few days the next week. The Protection Operations agent in L.A. would be pulling more than seven of the agents, including me, from the surveillance to stand post at the ranch. Continuing this surveillance with four agents wasn't going to work.

The case agent finally decided that if Audie loaded any boxes into the station wagon and started to leave, we would do a traffic stop on him and hopefully get a consent search or enough for a search warrant. His hope was Audie would be transporting counterfeit notes in the Ford station wagon. It wasn't much, but it was all we had. If we could just develop some good probable cause for a search warrant on the print shop, we'd be set! We knew Audie was printing counterfeit inside the shop, but how were we going to prove that?

If we could just get a peek inside the shop that might just be all we'd need.

We'd been on this surveillance for four or five days by now, living off fast food, and most of us hadn't shaved during that time. We were all looking pretty haggard. It was hot in L.A. that summer, and Audie had a screen door on the front door to his shop. We noticed that he kept the front door open and the screen door closed during business hours. The place wasn't air-conditioned and running an AB Dick 1200 generates some heat.

One of the guys came up with a pretty good idea; why not have one of our guys pretend to be a street bum, a drunk and wander on over to Audie's front door? Street bums were common in L.A., as in any big city, and our "bum" might be able to see the press and some counterfeit notes without raising any suspicions.

One of the agents from the LAFO was a tall, skinny, lanky guy, he always reminded me of the actor Vincent Schiuvelli. The agent should have won an Academy Award for his performance that day, or at least, he should have been nominated. If anybody looked like a homeless street guy, it was Rob. And Rob really got into his character. He bought two pints of cheap bourbon and poured one bottle all over his clothes and gargled with it. He jumped in to a Dumpster behind a restaurant and rolled around in the garbage. He stunk to high heaven.

Rob came stumbling down Crenshaw Blvd, staggering back a forth on the sidewalk. The pedestrians were aghast. When Rob got to Audie's print shop, he collapsed against the wall, just inches from the front screen door. He'd lift that paper bag and take a sip of whiskey every now and then and mumble incoherently. The agent in the surveillance van was dying laughing as he described the scene to the rest of us on the radio. It was classic! Every few minutes, Rob would get up and try to peek into the shop, and then sit back down with his back against the storefront wall. Finally, Audie came out to see who and what this guy was. Just because he was a counterfeiter didn't mean old Audie wasn't a compassionate guy. Audie kept trying to talk Rob into getting on the next bus that would stop just down the block and head north. There weren't very many white homeless drunks on Crenshaw in South Central and it seemed like Audie was worried for Rob's safety. "You're gonna get killed around here, white boy; get outta here!" he told Rob. Finally, Rob got what he needed and staggered north on Crenshaw.

Rob was able to see inside the shop and he saw the AB Dick behind the counter running a mile a minute. He couldn't really see any counterfeit notes, the cylinder of the printer was spinning to fast, but he could see green spinning by and the undeniable sounds of the cha-chunk of the printer. The case agent was able to take that information, along with all the other evidence we'd gathered about Audie's operation, and got a US magistrate to sign the warrant.

We hit the place as soon as the judge signed the warrant. When we burst into the shop, Audie had the press running full speed, and he was printing one-hundred-dollar bills. We found stacks of uncut sheets with four images per sheet of counterfeit one hundreds. The printer paper trough was full of paper. And son of a bitch, it ran out of paper before we could find the off switch and shut her down.

Once we had all the evidence inventoried and secured at the LAFO, I drove three hours back to Las Vegas. When I got home I kissed the Redhead hello and good-bye, packed, and drove five hours west for an assignment in Santa Barbara. I loved standing post at President Reagan's ranch.

Chapter 8

A Biker Gang Reject

Ranch del Cielo was one beautiful place. It was located just north of the city of Santa Barbara, high up in the Santa Ynez Mountains. Most of us young agents from L.A. (and Las Vegas was part of the LAFO) were assigned an eight-hour shift as resident security during the President's extended visits. We worked the middle security perimeter around the main part of the ranch. This meant long hours outside, in the elements, and you were lucky to get thirty minutes of downtime in the Security Room to eat a sub sandwich and wash it down with Diet Coke. But I'm an outdoorsy type and that suited me just fine. I still had my eye on an assignment to PPD when I finished my tour in the desert and I was young enough to still be inspired working alongside those PPD agents.

One sunny afternoon, as I was standing a security post on the middle perimeter of the ranch, the Command Post alerted all of us that President and Mrs. Reagan were commencing a horseback ride. It wasn't long after the radio call that I saw them in the pasture just below my position, riding horses from my left (back toward the barn) to my right and the beautiful green hills dotted with scrub oak trees. I looked back to my left and saw a group of about five agents keeping their horses a respectable distance behind the President. As I watched the PPD agents riding horses with President Reagan, little did I know that in less than six years I'd be riding horses with a different President of the United States...

* * *

Campaign or no campaign, in Las Vegas the crime never stopped. We were getting a lot of raised notes in the office lately. A raised note is an altered genuine note "raised" to a higher denomination. This is done by cutting the corners off a higher valued bill and taping or gluing them over the original notes corners, thereby "raising the value." Genuine US currency is considered acceptable if the note has more than 50 percent still intact. So a crook could cut the corners off one side of a one-hundred-dollar bill, then make the one hundred look like it had been torn at the edges, take it to a bank and the bank would give you a replacement one hundred dollar bill. The ripped currency was shipped to the Federal Reserve to be destroyed as mutilated currency. This type of counterfeit note, and it was considered counterfeit by the statute, was hard to pass. If the recipient took the time to actually look at the altered raised note, they might realize George Washington is on the one-dollar bill, not the one hundred dollar bill.

Generally speaking we didn't put much time into these raised note investigations. A crook altering notes this way was usually a juvenile; plus, not many US Attorneys would consider prosecuting this type of counterfeiting. But this was Las Vegas and we had a very aggressive US Attorney's office. Our office was getting flooded with raised notes and all of them were being passed at dimly light local bars/casinos.

Most of these neighborhood bars had no clue as to who passed the raised note and the information we got from a bank on counterfeit wasn't very specific as to what day and time the note was passed. Interviewing bartenders was a shot in the dark. But if you don't ask, you'll never find out.

These local bars were our "cheeseburger casinos" so one day I suggested we have lunch at one of the victim bars near East Tropicana and Eastern Avenue. After finishing up a really good cheeseburger—perhaps the best one yet—I walked over to a bartender, identified myself, and asked about the counterfeit bill passed there last week.

"Yeah, I know the guy that passed that shit. His name's Jeff Hunt. He used to come in regularly. But I haven't seen him in awhile," the bartender told me. "The next time I see him, he owes me a hundred bucks. Oh, and he's a real shithead…always bragging about his Hell's Angels buddies. Claims he once was one." The bartender gave me a good description of the suspect. I told him that if Hunt came back in to act like nothing was amiss and call me. I now had a suspect and a pretty good description; I just needed to find him.

* * *

The LVMPD had a very detailed computer database that contained basic information about folks who had been arrested or came in contact with a Vegas cop. The information in this database included just about everybody who lived in Vegas and half of the tourists who didn't comply with the law in one-way or another. Most of these entries had an accompanying photo, copies of which we could easily access. The database also had information on anyone who applied for work at one of the many casinos in Las Vegas and Clark County, Nevada.

To work for a casino, one had to get a card clearing them to do so from the PD. The PD would fingerprint the casino worker and run them for any wants and warrants, before issuing this work card. I guess casinos had standards. I don't know what those standards were and they must have not been too stringent, because we arrested a few casino workers in the four years I worked in Las Vegas.

* * *

Donnie walked into my office one afternoon; he'd just been assigned a letter writer case. It seemed a blackjack dealer at the Landmark Hotel and Casino didn't like President Reagan's policies, so he wrote him a nice letter and closed with, "I'm gonna rip your lungs out and stab you in the heart…a thousand times." Donnie said he had called the casino security office and the guy was working that afternoon, "Let's go see what makes him tick."

After explaining the situation to the security manager, the security team went and pulled him off his blackjack table and brought him to us. He was a white male, mid-thirties, a nice clean-cut looking fellow. Not the average nut case we ran into who liked to make threats or write letters to the White House. Maybe he just had a beef with the President and he chose the wrong words to express his anger. He willingly took the afternoon off and we drove him to our office.

This guy was hard to figure out. He sure seemed like your average Joe and he was extremely cooperative. He answered all our questions seemingly content with the situation—which was also very odd. If two Secret Service agents walked into my place of employment and told my boss I had written a threatening letter to the President, I'd be a little pissed off. Not Johnny Blackjack...he was calm, cool and collected. And a little happy, all smiles you know?

We took a break and stepped into Donnie's office. Donnie wanted to have him committed for forty-eight hours, to let the professionals evaluate his brain. "I don't know Donnie," I said, "He seems okay to me." Donnie agreed but he felt there was something just not right with the guy.

We went back in the interview room to continue our chat. Donnie mentioned something about the air force and Johnny Blackjack suddenly got excited. He went off on a tangent about spaceships flying over the desert north of Las Vegas. He said he'd climbed up Mormon Mountain and peered over the other side and he'd seen them. "Yep! Yep! Yep! I saw them spaceships!" And then, the next minute he was calm again, discussing Reagan's policies and why he disagreed with them. We were back to having a normal conversation.

Okay. He's nuts; must be bipolar: up and down, up and down.

It took us forever to convince him that we needed to take him to the hospital to have a doctor examine him. He was not going. It wasn't like he was physically refusing to go, he continued to be very cordial, but he just insisted his health—physical and mental health—were fine. Two hours later, we finally got him in the car and to the hospital.

He sat on the examination table, still not quite realizing what was happening to him. All those iron barred doors that kept opening for us and then closing behind us were meant to keep him there. As we escorted him into the psychiatric examination room, Johnny Blackjack just kind of looked around in bewilderment, not saying much except, "Come on guys, do we have to do this?" We could tell he was scared.

The doctor asked him a few questions and then said to us, "Okay, fellas, thank you." As we started to walk out, retracing our steps through the iron barred doors, we could hear Johnny Blackjack down the hall yelling, "Hey, come on, guys. Don't leave me here! Please don't leave me here with all these nuts! Come on, guys! This is chicken shit."

Donnie and I didn't say a word until we got into his sedan. I looked over at him and he looked at me. Donnie let out a big sigh. "Holy shit," he said. "What would you do if two Secret Service agents dropped you off at a psychiatric hospital and left you there? What would your reaction be?"

"I would have said the exact same thing he just said to us," I replied. "I would have begged you not to leave me there." *That poor guy, what if he's not really nuts? If he's not, he's going to have a fun two days!*

The next day the doctor from the psychiatric hospital called Donnie to thank us for bringing him in. "He's been admitted before and diagnosed with paranoid schizophrenia, with bipolar tendencies," he said.

Donnie came running into my office, "Thank God." He laughed, "He's *nuts!*"

* * *

I got to work on trying to identify my raised note suspect. I found two guys in the LVMPD database with the exact name, description and about the correct age. I got photos from the PD and made up two separate photos spreads, one with one Jeff Hunt and five similar looking males and the other with the other Jeff Hunt, and five similar looking white males. The bartender who'd told me his name had no problem picking out the suspect from one of the photo spreads. "That's him," he said as he pointed to the picture of Jeff Hunt.

The LVMPD database didn't list an address for my Jeff Hunt and finding him would not be easy. But I got lucky one morning when the LVMPD dispatcher called our office to report a motel manager called 9-1-1. A maid found "counterfeit money" in room 203 of the No-Tell Motel out by the airport. A guest named Jeff Hunt was registered to the room.

The three of us went to the motel, knocked on the door to room 203 and woke him up. We got him handcuffed and sat him on the bed. He was cussing up a storm; threatening to kill us…this guy was fucking mean. I asked him for a consent search of the room.

"Fuck you!" he said. That seemed to be his favorite response to our questions. Between the cussing and spitting, we decided it was time for this guy to go. The Beaver called LVMPD for assistance and we loaded him in the back of a black-and-white for the trip to the Clark County Jail. The Beaver rode with the cop and Donnie and I did a plain view search of the room. X-Acto knives and Scotch tape were sitting on the dresser. *Bingo!* I called T.J. and he said, "Let's get a search warrant."

After I got the search warrant signed we went back to the secured room (we put a "Clam-shell" lock on the room door and advised the motel manager to keep all his employees away from the room) and executed the search warrant. Tucked away in a dresser drawer we found two one-hundred-dollar bills with the corners shaved off at an angle, and a bunch of one-dollar bills. But that was about it. With the X-Acto knife and Scotch tape, I had my guy. "Hey, Donnie," I said, "Do you think this qualifies for a seizure of a counterfeit plant?"

"I don't see why not," he said to me. "It's all in how you write it up!"

Hunt decided to go to trial on the three-count indictment for passing counterfeit notes. I guess I couldn't blame him; he had a rap sheet as long as my arm—violent crimes, armed robbery, biker gang stuff. I had located three really good eyewitnesses who were willing to testify. All three were bartenders who remembered Hunt clearly; two were women and the other was the guy from the bar on East Tropicana.

During trial preparation, the AUSA decided he wanted to meet with the witnesses at the scene where the notes were passed. He wanted to get a visual feel for the events. I made arrangements with each of the bartenders to meet us at their place of employment and the scene of the crimes. One bartender really made a lasting impression on both of us. She was a cute blonde, a very petite woman, but very confident of herself, as you might imagine a woman would be who dealt with drunkards every day. You could tell she didn't put up with any bullshit from anybody. When we left the bar, the AUSA commented that she would be the star witness. Her testimony and her vivid recollection of Hunt's actions during and after he passed that counterfeit note were outstanding. "She'll seal the guilty verdict," the AUSA told me.

During all of the court hearings leading up to the trial, Hunt was his usual mean, spitting-mad self. He was very uncooperative with the court and answered most questions posed by the judge with a "fuck this" or "fuck that" remark. He didn't pay much attention to his assistant federal public defender. Hunt was just one mean-spirited human being. He liked to just give you a piercing, hateful stare with his jaw clenched.

The first phase of a jury trial was the selection of the twelve men or women who would decide the verdict. As our trial began, the courtroom behind us was filled with prospective jurors. The judge went through each of the jurors who wished to be excused from jury duty, approving or disapproving this guy or that gal. Some of the excuses people came up with were just everyday stuff—an elderly parent to care for, kids in school, sick kids, a job...*really?* *A job?*

One older guy did seem to have a legitimate reason; he was the project manager for the restoration of the USS Missouri battleship in Pearl Harbor, Hawaii. He had to leave for Pearl Harbor the following day and his absence would delay the restoration. The judge said, "Aloha" and the old guy said, "Mahalo" and he walked out of the courtroom.

Prosecutors are always nervous about jury selection and I was a little concerned too, but this wasn't my first jury trial. We had a solid case with three excellent witnesses and Hunt was such a mean bastard I couldn't imagine losing this verdict. But you never know about juries. You just never know.

* * *

The Beaver had a good, one-note counterfeit pass arrest that went to trial in US federal court in Las Vegas. Yes, a one-note pass. Again, we had a very aggressive US Attorney. That might not be the only federal arrest for a one-note pass and it might not be the only one-note pass that went to a jury trial, but you can bet there weren't many of those cases in the post-WWII history of the Secret Service.

The Beaver went out on a duty call to McCarran International Airport one night. It was late…it was always late, or early in the morning depending on your outlook on life. He called me, woke up the Redhead, and asked if I could go with him. This twentysomething high-roller wannabe from Phoenix was sitting in first class on his short flight to Vegas. A flight attendant saw him holding up a twenty-dollar bill to the overhead reading light and loudly bragging that it was counterfeit and you couldn't even tell.

The flight attendant did the right thing and had the pilot radio ahead to the Las Vegas airport and the LVMPD picked him up as he walked off the plane. He was sitting in handcuffs in the substation when we showed up. The cops did a search incident to arrest and found a small amount of cocaine in his suitcase. But he only had one counterfeit note. The Beaver advised him of his Miranda rights and he immediately said he wanted to speak to his attorney. A little disappointing for us, because working the case back to the source was always our hope, you know, turn this guy into a snitch and go do some real Secret Service investigative work.

The Duty AUSA told the Beaver to go ahead and put him in federal custody, we might be able to get him to cooperate after we talk with the assistant federal public defender. I was always amazed at how many defendants qualified for a public defender. They had to fill out a financial statement for the court and the magistrate would look it over and inevitably say you qualify. But yet when a defendant appeared in later court hearings and declared he was a businessman or whatever, no judge ever questioned his honesty on the financial affidavit. One of those mysteries of the judicial system, I guess.

The high-roller Wannabe refused to cooperate and the US Attorney's office proceeded with the trial. They had good witnesses, the Beaver got the flight attendant and he even found the passenger sitting next to the high-roller Wannabe. They had good testimony that the white powdery substance was indeed cocaine. The AUSA gave a good, rock-solid presentation of the evidence, it was one of those trials you just knew you would win.

The defense called one witness, Mr. High Roller. He took the stand and lied his ass off. His testimony directly contradicted the two eyewitnesses. He gave some lame excuse that he was passed the note as change, probably at the Phoenix airport lounge when he bought a cocktail before the flight left for Las Vegas. He knew it was counterfeit and intended to turn it in to the first policemen he saw in Las Vegas.

The Beaver had indicted him for one count of possession of counterfeit currency and one count of possession of cocaine. Possessing the counterfeit was a felony, a big time twenty-year felony. The cocaine amount was so small it resulted in a federal misdemeanor violation. A jury doesn't know if the charges in an indictment are felonies or misdemeanors, at least the judge does not tell them whether a charge is a felony or a misdemeanor. So the jury comes back, not guilty on possessing counterfeit currency and guilty on possession of cocaine.

We were floored by that injustice. After the trial, the Beaver asked one of the jurors, "Why did you find him not guilty on possessing the counterfeit? Our evidence was overwhelming." This nice old lady looked at the Beaver and said, "The defendant seemed like such a nice young fellow and we knew he was lying, so we split the difference and gave him a break for possessing the counterfeit and thought the cocaine was much more serious so we voted guilty on that count."

Again...you never know about juries.

* * *

We had our twelve, and the Hunt trial was set to start the next morning in US district court for Las Vegas at nine in the morning, with the AUSA presenting our evidence and our witnesses. The Redhead took the day off so she could come and watch the trial. The courtroom was empty, no visitors in the gallery and as we were about to start opening statements for the jury, in walks the Redhead. As she took a seat in the gallery, I noticed Hunt glaring; that hateful piercing stare and overheard him asked his public defender, "Who the fuck is that?"

At the first recess, I waited until the jury was excused to the jury room and Hunt was escorted out of the courtroom to the US

Marshals holding cell, before I approached the Redhead. "Do me a favor Sweetie," I said, "Do not acknowledge me in the courtroom, and do not even look at me. I don't want this guy to have any inkling you are my wife. He's a vindictive type and we don't need that." The Redhead understood immediately.

This was not the first time I'd admonished her to ignore me. One Saturday afternoon we were at the local grocery store, when I simply disappeared on her. I spied a guy I'd once arrested down one of the aisles when we were walking in. He was coming straight at us; I pivoted and walked right out to the car. When the Redhead showed up with a basket full of bags she was pissed off. "I made three laps around that store trying to find you!" she said. Once I explained my disappearance to her, she got it.

The AUSA had me testify to establish the legal aspects of the investigation and the eventual identity of the defendant, as the guy who committed the crime. The bartenders were next up and the AUSA saved Blondie for the afternoon session. She would be our last witness. The AUSA led her through the crime, perfectly. She remembered everything in great detail. The most dramatic testimony was when, after she recognized the note as counterfeit and confronted Hunt; he jumped up from his bar stool and started in with his mean, tough guy persona. Was she afraid of him?

"Absolutely," this small petite blonde said. "I was scared to death! He angrily pointed his finger at me and said if I called the police he would kill me! His exact words were he had an Uzi and he'd come back and use it on me."

I looked at Hunt and he was giving her the glare, the meanest glare I'd ever seen. I glanced at the jury and they noticed it too. The AUSA asked if she believed his statement; that he had an Uzi and would come back. "Absolutely," she said again. "He's the scariest man I've ever seen."

The defense called me as their only witness. I was shocked. *Really? Me?* On cross-examination the public defender had questioned my photo spread and now he really tore into me. It was all he had and you can't blame him for trying. He was trying to establish some reasonable doubt in the minds of the jury, that I had the wrong Jeff Hunt. This was the same PD who'd defended Mark Matthews, had me do a police lineup, and then was dumb enough to pick the other prisoners for the line up, eliminating any argument that the police line up was rigged against his defendant. So, I wasn't too worried. The AUSA did an outstanding job on his cross-examination of me and we sealed the deal. The Jeff Hunt who passed those raised notes was sitting right there at the defense table.

The jury went out for deliberation and we headed to the AUSA's office to wait for a call from the clerk that the jury had reached a decision. I was confident, but like all prosecutors, the AUSA was worried. "Don't worry," I told him, "This is a done deal."

We had hardly sat down in his office when the clerk called. The jury had reached a verdict and back to the courtroom we went. They say a quick verdict favors the prosecution, and some say a quick verdict favors the defense. This quick verdict was guilty on all three counts of the indictment. It probably took the jury longer to pick a foreman than to reach a verdict.

As I've said before, in those days, Vegas was a law and order town. Judges actually sentenced defendants to some real jail time. I had a great respect for those judges, and the fact that they were willing to hand down hard sentences validated what I did everyday.

* * *

The US district court judge in the Hunt case was the same judge the Beaver had in a credit card case that went to trial. And in that case the assistant federal public defender was once again, the same lawyer who (tried) to defend Matthews and Hunt.

One of the government's witnesses was an LVMPD cop. Beaver's AUSA called Officer Friendly to the stand. The cop walked into the courtroom in full uniform. He was looking sharp! Neatly pressed uniform with spit-polished shoes, and his revolver in his holster. The officer took his seat in the witness chair and the public defender jumps up and screams, "That man is *armed*, Your Honor!"

The judge, without missing a beat, and very calmly, I might add, peered over his reading glasses, perched on the end of his nose and said, "The more good guys with guns the better...please proceed."

So I had high hopes that Mr. Mean-As-A-Rattlesnake Hunt would get the maximum sentence of twenty years.

* * *

At his sentencing hearing a few months later, Hunt was his usual mean self. "Anything to say Mr. Hunt before I impose the sentence?" the judge had asked.

"Fuck you!" Hunt had snarled.

The US district court judge sentenced Hunt to eighteen years in the federal penitentiary. Eighteen frickin' years for passing raised notes. It wasn't the full twenty, but it was damn close. Unfortunately, the federal public defender appealed Hunt's lengthy sentence to the 9th Circuit Court of Appeals. The appellate court ruled in Hunt's favor and he ended up only doing thirty-four months at Club Fed.

Chapter 9

"Looked a Lot Like Eddie Murphy"

I went back out on the campaign trail with Senator Simon. He was actually the front-runner for a while, but faded into the pack after Iowa and New Hampshire. When he skipped the Super Tuesday primaries, I figured he was about done. Simon finally pulled out in April 1988 and he returned to the Senate. Senator Simon, his wife, daughter, and son were some of the nicest people I have ever met, and I've met a bunch. I remember seeing them on an airport tarmac somewhere down the campaign trail later that year. The senator and his family saw me, took the time to stop and asked how I was doing. And I ran into them years later in Illinois and I'll be darned if they didn't remember me and again take the time to say hello. Small-town folks...you can't beat their hospitality.

After the Democratic convention was held, former Massachusetts governor Michael Dukakis was nominated as the presidential candidate to run against Reagan's incumbent vice president George H. W. Bush, and he chose Senator Lloyd Benson of Texas as his running mate. I was assigned to Senator Benson's detail for the remainder of the campaign season. I did those twenty-one-day rotations all the way through to the first Tuesday in November. I really loved working on the details. The Redhead wasn't so crazy about me being gone so much of that year, but she enjoyed the bigger paychecks.

When I was a GS-9, I wasn't making much money and the overtime we got paid was a big help. Early on in my career, a senior agent once told me the key to keeping the wife happy about your heavy travel schedule was to break the news to her the correct way. He said he always started a conversation with his wife, not with, "I have to go on the road again," but with, "I'm going to make a lot of overtime next week." I used that line extensively the next few years. I added some additional lines as she started to catch on to my ruse, "You know that new couch you been thinking about? Well, next month I think we'll be able to afford it."

I was back in Las Vegas after one of the rotations with Senator Benson. It was a hot, lazy Vegas Saturday afternoon; the Redhead and I were lounging around and relaxing at home. I was the duty agent and the telephone rang. It was our after-hours answering service. The operator told me an investigator with First Data Resources (FDR) in Omaha, Nebraska, was on the line and he wanted to speak to an agent. "Put him on the line," I said as I glanced at the Redhead. She had that frown on her face that said, "There goes my weekend with my husband."

The investigator told me he'd been tracking two suspects who were using falsely applied for credit cards to bilk banks out of big bucks. The suspects were in Las Vegas and they were racking up the fraudulent purchases and cash advances on numerous credit cards. He said the security manager at Neiman Marcus had just discovered both had been in his store and I should call him for some more information. The investigator gave me a laundry list of casinos and shops the suspect had hit that day.

I called the security manager and arranged to meet him, then I called the Beaver and we headed down to the Fashion Show Mall. The store security manager told us that a black female and a black male were in the store and made high dollar amount purchases with stolen credit cards. The pair had "Texas Department of Identification" cards to match the names on the credit cards. He said they spoke with an odd British accent.

These suspects had Nigerian credit card fraudster written all over them. In the late eighties and even the early nineties the Secret Service nationwide and the three of us in Las Vegas noticed a huge increase in fraudulent credit card transactions. In Las Vegas, that resulted in us arresting Nigerians from either Houston or Dallas doing cash advances with Visa, MasterCard and American Express cards at casinos. The Nigerians were using fictitious "Texas Department of Identification" cards as identification. There was no such agency in the state of Texas.

* * *

We had been called to Bally's Hotel and Casino numerous times and the three of us had hauled a lot of Nigerians out of Bally's in handcuffs. Why Bally's? Bally's was located on Las Vegas Boulevard and Flamingo Road; I guess it was the first stop for them when they came onto the Strip from the airport. Who knows? I had a conversation with the Bally's casino cage manager on one investigation and told her the "Texas Department of Identification" was a dead giveaway that the credit card was stolen or obtained fraudulently, because there was no such agency. Consequently, anytime a cash advance was attempted with that type of identification, Bally's security grabbed the individual(s) and called us.

Not very long after I had alerted the cage manager of this scam, Bally's called us one night and reported a black male, with a British accent was attempting to get an eight-hundred-dollar cash advance on a MasterCard credit card. He presented a "Texas Department of Identification" card with the same name as that on the credit card. He claimed his name was John Rhodes.

Bally's had run the credit card transaction through the system and they'd been given an authorization number—thus, the cash advance was approved. If a merchant received an authorization for the charge, very seldom would they question the transaction. The credit card companies stressed to their merchants that clerks should be trained to spot a counterfeit card, but a credit card obtained with a false application was a genuine card issued by the bank.

So now I'm sitting in the security office at Bally's with a guy who is upset because he's been grabbed by Bally's security, for what he claims is no reason. He's a little pissed off. The federal credit card statue, Title 18 United States Code Section 1029, has a one-thousand-dollar threshold, so unless I can document at least a thousand dollars in fraud, he hasn't violated that statue and I can not arrest him for that. However, I know his Texas identification is fictitious, it is counterfeit, and so I could arrest him for that. But I knew Donnie's old adage "You can bet they aren't who they say they are, and you can bet it is not the first time they've done it" was as true as the Vegas sky is blue.

I advised Rhodes of his Miranda rights and started the interview with some innocuous questions about his personal information.

Name? "John Rhodes."

Address? "Inglewood Boulevard, Redondo Beach, California."

Place of birth? "St. Thomas, US Virgin Islands."

Occupation? "Computer programmer."

Employer? "Eastern Airlines."

St. Thomas, US Virgin Islands. Nigerians typically claimed to be from the Virgin Islands, because it explained their British-type accent and the US Virgin Islands are a US territory, therefore, they could claim US citizenship.

I knew this guy was lying to me, but I played dumb and then I led him through the transaction "Is this your credit card?"

"Yes"

"How did you get it?"

"I made an application to First National Bank of Chicago."

"How many credit cards to you have?"

"This MasterCard and a Visa credit card."

"Did you present this credit card at the casino cage and asked for an eight-hundred-dollar cash advance?"

"Yes."

"Did you sign for this cash advance? Is this your signature on the credit card transaction receipt?"

"Yes."

"Where did you get this ID?"

"Texas."

"I thought you lived in California?"

He paused. I could see the wheels spinning inside his head. He knows I just caught him in a lie. "Okay, I went to Houston and bought it from a guy. He had numerous state driver's licenses and identification cards."

"How much did you pay for it?"

"Twenty dollars."

"Why did you need a fictitious ID?"

"Okay, I'm not really a computer programmer for Eastern Airlines."

Just another illegal alien living in the shadows. And scamming banks and the government out of every penny they could get.

"What is your real name? Where were you really born?" I continued.

"I would like to speak to an attorney," he said. I placed him under arrest for violation of Title 18 United States Code Section 1028, Section A4: "Whoever uses a false identification document to defraud the United States." It was thin, but the First National Bank of Chicago is a federally insured bank, thus the nexus to the United States.

Back in the 1980s most banks didn't have a 24/7 security hotline for cops to make an inquiry with the bank about a suspicious credit card transaction, so early that next morning I got on the telephone with a fraud investigator from the bank in Chicago. The investigator told me over two thousand dollars had been charged to that credit card, including a cash advance the day before (the day I interviewed him at Bally's) at a Las Vegas casino for fifteen hundred bucks. The investigator said records indicated Rhodes had ten credit cards issued to him. The total credit card fraud, and the loss to the issuing banks was greater than fifty thousand dollars. One phone call and I had fifty thousand dollars in fraud.

Rhodes was very uncooperative with the court. He refused to be interviewed by pretrial services, an arm of the court that helps the judge determine the defendant's financial situation, criminal record, and his eligibility for bail. He obviously knew he was going to be deported and he was trying to delay the inevitable. A sharp special agent with US Immigration finally got the truth out of him when he couldn't answer some simple questions about the US Virgin Islands. He came to the United States on a student visa...and just forgot to go back to Nigeria after college didn't work out for him.

A very typical scenario of illegal aliens. The good, old student visa trick! It worked like a charm.

* * *

The Neiman Marcus security manager said when the woman was making her purchase, the store clerk had kindly asked if she wanted to open a Neiman Marcus credit card account. A typical question a store clerk asks customers to this very day. Open an account today and you get an extra 10 percent off your purchase.

"Of course," the woman answered. "I'd love to open a Neiman Marcus credit card account." *I mean, come on! A fraudster can never have too many illegally obtained credit cards, right?* Like I said earlier, why rob a bank with a gun? Oh, and the Mister? Yes, of course he'd like an extra 10 percent off today, too!

What Mr. and Mrs. Credit Card Fraudsters didn't know was that when they used the account numbers of their fraudulently obtained credit cards that they were using for the purchases at Neiman Marcus on the credit application, a sharp investigator from FDR in Omaha was on to them. He had placed an alert to "call me before extending credit" on the credit report. As Mr. and Mrs. Credit Card Fraudsters wandered the store waiting for their extra 10 percent off to materialize, the security manager was on the telephone with FDR. He confronted the two and they bolted immediately out the door onto Las Vegas Boulevard. The male grabbed the female's purse out of her hand and headed south as she headed north.

The security manager chased after them out onto the Strip, his head swiveling from south to north and north to south. He had to pick one and he went south in pursuit of the Mister. I was slightly impressed; running after a crook high on adrenaline and actually catching him is quite a feat.

Unfortunately a struggle ensued. Adrenaline is something powerful and the fear of going to jail can really get a crook's adrenaline pumping, especially when he is caught. So the Mister was able to wrestle free and disappeared into the throngs of tourists walking the Strip. But, I had to give the guy credit; it was a noble try by a dedicated security manager. I hope the guy got a raise.

Unfortunately, the security cameras didn't capture any good facial shots of the pair. That was always the case. I always wondered why in the hell they put security cameras high on the wall, usually in a corner, over looking the floor of a store. A good video or photo of the tops of heads of criminals doesn't do much good when a cop is looking for an unknown suspect. The clerks and the security manager couldn't give us much more than a description of their clothes, estimated age, race and gender. As the Beaver and I started to leave, I asked the security manager, "Is there anything else you can think of? Did they mention where they were staying? What hotel?"

"No," he said, "But you know, the guy looked a lot like Eddie Murphy."

We went by the casinos where they had gotten cash advances and gathered as much evidence as we could. I called the FDR investigator a couple of times later that afternoon in response to several pages from our after hours answering service. He indicated it appeared they were back together and hitting casinos in Glitter Gulch—the Union Plaza, the Lady Luck, and the Golden Nugget. He also told me they flew from Houston to Las Vegas using airline tickets bought with a stolen credit card. He discovered their return flight to Houston was leaving Las Vegas at two Sunday morning.

The Beaver and I went to the downtown casinos and it seemed we were just missing them by minutes. We canvassed other casinos downtown and spread the word with the security departments, providing the suspects description and MO. We were having zero luck finding these two, but we still had their departing flight to bank on. If they showed up.

We went to McCarran Airport around midnight and checked in with the airport cops. The Beaver and I walked toward the tram to get to the departure gate for the flight. Even in the eighties the Las Vegas airport was one busy place, handling millions of tourists dreaming of the big score at the Vegas casinos. But on that night it was pretty quiet and mostly deserted. As we walked toward the tram, we could see only two people waiting for the next tram. Two black males. One was tall and rather large, the second one was shorter. The closer we got, the more the short guy looked like Eddie Murphy. I nudged the Beaver. "There he is." We were in full-on arrest mode. That's our guy! We casually waited a few doors down from the two guys. No one else was getting on the tram. "Let's get him before he gets on the tram." We walked a little closer, ready to make our move. Wait! That's Eddie Murphy...that's the real Eddie Murphy! I'll be damn if it wasn't. "Good morning, Mr. Murphy."

We rode the tram out to the C gates with Mr. Murphy and, I guess, his bodyguard (the guy was huge). We went to the gate for the flight to Houston, waited and watched for Mr. and Mrs. Fraudster. Eventually, a black male and a black female, who matched the description, came to the gate. Beaver and I looked them over and both decided they had to be our suspects. We approached them and identified ourselves. I ask them their names. They both replied with a foreign accent, a British accent. We kindly asked them to accompany us to the PD substation at the airport. Mister Fraudster did look a little like Eddie Murphy.

They both played dumb during the initial stages of our interview. They pulled the typical trick, pleading innocence. "That's my credit card, that's my name, maybe I'm late with my monthly payment, but I've been out of town..." We had heard those excuses before. But the lady's purse had four different credit cards in four different names and two "Texas Department of Identification" cards with names to match two of the credit cards. These credit cards matched some of the fraudulent transactions made in Las Vegas that the FDR fraud investigator had told me about.

We booked them into the Clark County Jail and I swore out an affidavit with John and Jane Doe arrest warrants. They followed the pattern and refused to cooperate with the US magistrate. I'm not sure if the court ever did determine their real names. Both ended up pleading guilty to the indictment and they were sentenced to only a few months each in a federal penitentiary. The US district court judge ordered they be deported at the conclusion of their sentences. I wouldn't be surprised if they both lived in Houston.

* * *

There's an old saying in law enforcement: We only catch the dumb ones. I don't necessarily believe that, but I do know the dumb ones just make it easier. Take Ahmed Kalahi, for example, another Nigerian who made the mistake of trying to obtain a cash advance with a Visa credit card at Bally's. By the time Ahmed showed up, the cashiers at Bally's casino cage were really in tune with false identification. Kalahi presented the Visa credit card and a Rhode Island driver's license to obtain a fifteen-hundred-dollar cash advance. The cashier compared the Rhode Island driver's license against an "Identification Guide" booklet that had photos and descriptions of state issued driver's licenses. It didn't match, so she asked Kalahi his date of birth. The Rhode Island identification listed Kalahi's date of birth as August 19, 1955; Kalahi told the cashier his birthday was April 21, 1954. Oops! Casino security grabbed him and called me.

Kalahi told me that the Visa credit card was his and that he'd applied to Bank of America for the card. Bank of America was one of the few major banks with a 24/7 police hotline; I excused myself from the Bally's security interview room and placed a telephone call to them. The bank records indicated Kalahi had applied for the card and it had been issued to him. The security investigator asked to speak with Kalahi. She asked him his social security number... he fumbled that one too. Time to go to jail, Mr. Kalahi.

Kalahi told me he was a taxi driver in Washington, DC, and that's all he would tell me. He refused to answer any personal history questions and he refused to sign the FBI fingerprint cards. The US magistrate released him on bail, which was a bit of a surprise. But I'll be damned if he didn't return to Las Vegas for his change of plea hearing.

Change of plea hearings are held before a US district court judge, and it just so happened that the judge assigned to the case was in Washington, DC, for meetings. By pure coincidence, on his return flight to Las Vegas, the judge was sitting in the seat next to the defendant. And apparently, Mr. Khalil was one of those airline passengers that just love to tell their seatmate their life story. Somewhere over flyover country the judge realized his seatmate was coming to Las Vegas to plead guilty to credit card fraud in his courtroom.

* * *

Donnie, the Beaver, and I were arresting so many Nigerians it was completely unbelievable. I was discussing a Nigerian case with an investigator with a major bank and she told me her bank had started a database of addresses used by fraudsters, mainly Nigerians, to help the bank combat their fraud losses. When the bank received an application and the address of the applicant matched a known address of a previous falsely applied for credit card, they would flag the application for further inquiries to ensure the bank was issuing a credit card to a legitimate customer and not a fraudster.

After our call, the wheels in my head started spinning—*let's set up a sting!*

I placed a phone call to another investigator with another major nationwide bank and he told me his department was doing the same thing with the known addresses from false applications for credit cards. I went into Donnie's office and ran my plan by him and he thought it was a great idea.

If we rent out a ballroom at a major Las Vegas casino, we could set up a "processing" station of Secret Service agents, other law enforcement agents, and bank investigators to verify a credit card as falsely obtained by the Nigerians we targeted. We send out mass mailings to known addresses used by Nigerians, tell them they won something "special," something so tempting they couldn't turn it down, tell them to report to the "Flamingo Room" at the "Whatever Hotel and Casino" on a specific date at a specific time.

We tell them all they have to do to claim this tremendous prize is present their Visa or MasterCard with their identification and they win!

Donnie and I briefed the boss on the sting. He actually thought we could iron out all the details and pull it off, but we were going to need money and manpower from headquarters to set this up and make it work. "Write up a detailed proposal, addressed to the SAIC of Fraud Division," he told me. "I'll sign it and we'll send it up the chain. All they can say is no."

The boss said we should not start making any contacts with the US Attorney's office just yet, even though without their blessing this sting was a pipe dream; and don't contact any banks; don't contact anyone about participation because if we can't secure funding and a commitment from Fraud Division we would be wasting our time.

Donnie and I put together a very detailed plan on how we envisioned this sting going down, how we could lure the known fraudsters to the ballroom, which statutes they could be arrested for, the estimated financial investment needed, and all the logistics to make the sting a success. And to our surprise, the Fraud Division actually considered my proposal. The Fraud Division ASAIC flew out to Las Vegas and we had a meeting to discuss the sting.

It always comes down to money and Fraud Division decided funds were not available. In the middle of a presidential campaign money was tight. "But," the ASAIC of the Fraud Division told me, "we like your initiative out there in the desert. Keep up the good work."

* * *

Bally's and a few other casinos had become very adept at spotting counterfeit identification documents. And there was a good reason for that. When a cashier finished a shift and counted out the till, it all had to balance out, and any shortage resulted in the cashier losing the money from his or her paycheck.

It was the same for those cute change girls wandering around the casino floor. At the end of their shift, if the till didn't add up, they were out the money. One night the Beaver and I responded to a call from the Circus Circus Casino. Security had one in custody for passing a counterfeit twenty-dollar bill. This knucklehead tried to pass the counterfeit to a change girl and she spotted it as bad immediately. A casino is a dumb place to pass a counterfeit because change girls, casino cashiers, and dealers handle a large amount of cash daily. They are like bank tellers...counting bills constantly. Remember, a genuine FRN is printed by the intaglio method and that gives the note a rough, three-dimensional feel. Counterfeits printed by an offset press have the ink flat on the

TIM WOOD

paper...they feel smooth to the touch. A seasoned cashier or bank
teller doesn't even have to look at a bill to tell it's counterfeit...
they can feel it.

This change girl confronted the passer and he took off running
for the front door. She took off right after him, hollering and
screaming for help from security. He made it out to Las Vegas
Boulevard, but she didn't stop at the door. No sir, she ran him down,
with two overweight Circus Circus security officers trying to catch
up to them. This gal tackled the bad guy on the sidewalk!

It turned out he and his girlfriend had twenty thousand dollars
in counterfeit twenties in the trunk of their car. We arrested both of
them...and all because that change girl wasn't about to be cheated
out of twenty bucks when her shift was over.

* * *

The 1988 campaign began to wind down: I was working the
shift on the Benson detail the night he had the one vice presidential
debate with Senator Dan Quayle, the Republican VP nominee.
I was holding a security post off of stage left, out of sight of the
audience and TV cameras. When Senator Benson spoke his famous
line about Senator Quayle, which was something like "I knew Jack
Kennedy, Senator. And *you* are *no* Jack Kennedy!" The audience
roared with laughter and I knew immediately the media would take
that thirty-second sound bite and make it famous, and boy did they
ever! Anytime, even to this day, when media pundits are discussing
Dan Quayle, that sound bite gets mentioned.

After the election loss of Dukakis and Benson to Bush and
Quayle in November the Secret Service ended protection for Senator
Benson. I remember Senator Benson as a fine Texas gentleman, he
was a super-nice guy, and he once gave me a tip on cooking ears of
fresh corn. "Stick 'em in the microwave with a splash of water. Set

124

the timer for two minutes per ear. They will turn out perfect." The Redhead still uses the "Benson Method" to this day.

I was glad to get back to Vegas and my criminal cases. That campaign was a great learning experience for a young agent and I found I really enjoyed the protection mission of the Secret Service. Every now and then you'd run into an agent who hated protection, they just wanted to work criminal cases. I discovered I absolutely loved both missions equally. I couldn't wait for my assignment to a permanent detail and I still had PPD in my sights.

Chapter 10

Nigerians in My Backyard

Not all Nigerian fraudsters were transient to Vegas; we had a couple of guys I was chasing after who were local residents. I'd received some information from a Las Vegas bank fraud investigator that four checking accounts had been opened in four different names at four different branches of the bank. The names on all four accounts were foreign, African sounding last names with common English first names such as John or Charles; typical of Nigerians. Whoever was opening the accounts was kiting checks into the accounts.

Check kiting is a simple scheme utilizing the processing delay between the bank where the check was deposited and when the check clears the bank of origin. The fraudster will deposit checks drawn on closed accounts, inflating their checking account and get access to those funds before the original bank can notify the depositing bank that the original check was worthless due to nonsufficient funds.

The investigator told me that bank surveillance photos of ATM transactions showed the same black male using all four accounts. Bank employees at a fifth branch believed the ATM photos resembled a new customer known as Charles Musigbe.

I did a drive-by of the address provided by the investigator and wrote down the license plate numbers of two cars sitting in the driveway. One was registered to Charles Musigbe and the other car was registered to Matthew Musigbe.

Charles Musigbe was of record in the LVMPD database for an application to work in a casino and I was able to get a good photo. The photo from the PD and the photos from the ATM transactions were very close. Those damn ATM photos were grainy black and white in those days, and it never failed that the angle of the lens was always off-kilter just enough that you couldn't get a really good look at the face. But, I thought, *"If it ain't him, it's his fucking brother."*

A different bank in Las Vegas called and reported a very similar case. This investigator, who just happened to be the Redhead, told me a man opened a checking account with a Nigerian passport and a Trinidad driver's license. The driver's license number was written in the format of a US Social Security number. This should have been a red flag for the teller who opened the account. If people would just take the time to stop and think, *"Wait a minute, why does this customer have a Nigerian passport and a Trinidad driver's license?"* You would think they would have at least asked the customer about it! It always seemed pretty obvious to me. But, then again, I guess most people don't think they are about to be scammed. Do you think they have US Social Security numbers in the country of Trinidad? He had been kiting checks through the account and the loss to this bank was over eight thousand dollars in five days. *What? She couldn't tell me about this over our morning coffee?*

The name on this account was John Musigbe. Musigbe was depositing checks from a closed account at an Atlanta bank. He was using his ATM card to withdraw available funds before the Redhead's bank was notified by the Atlanta bank that the account was closed. Musigbe was also writing checks at local merchants and using his ATM card as a "check guarantee card."

I canvassed some of the merchants where he wrote bad checks and found a couple of witnesses that positively identified Musigbe from a photo spread. People, in this case, witnesses, remember other people if there is something unusual about that person…something that stands out. All of my witnesses recalled the transactions because of the guy's accent and his mannerisms. He was a foreigner. And he was buying high-dollar items. Clerks tend to remember that kind of stuff.

It was starting to look like I was into a Nigerian fraud ring living in my backyard.

I got a telephone call from a Las Vegas US Customs special agent. US Customs at JFK Airport in New York had intercepted a package mailed from Lagos, Nigeria, addressed to a John Alitio at the same address as Musigbe. Three Nigerian passports, official-looking documents, three different names, all with a photograph of Musigbe. It was time for a controlled delivery and a search warrant.

* * *

We did a lot of controlled deliveries when we worked a credit card fraud case. One of the most common ways for fraudsters to use their stolen credit cards was to purchase merchandise over the telephone and have it delivered to their homes or even vacant homes. We'd worked a fraud case in L.A. where the suspect would find vacant homes—perhaps homes listed for sale and the owner's had already moved out. The suspect would hide out where he could watch for the UPS man leave the package on the front and then he'd casually walk up and grab the box.

We received outstanding cooperation from UPS, FedEx, and the other delivery services with these cases. Donnie, the Beaver, and I took turns working these "undercover" assignments; they were always fun. I had dressed up like a UPS man so many times over the years I was half expecting to get a bill for union dues.

We always wore an UHF transmitter and a tape recorder when doing these controlled deliveries. If you went to trial it was good to have the crook on tape admitting he ordered the goods. You had to be careful about what you said to the unsuspecting crook. Everything on that tape is discoverable for the defense and I'm not talking about illegal things, such as entrapment, but more mundane things that a defense attorney could pounce on at trial to make you look incompetent. Defense attorneys will use anything to put doubt in a jury's mind.

Donnie had one of these fraud cases and the boss decided he wanted to get in on the fun. "Sure, boss, have at it! I'll take one of the surveillance positions down the street."

The boss put on the uniform and got in the delivery truck with the security manager, who was our driver. This particular case involved using stolen credit cards to order merchandise for delivery to a home. Thousands of dollars' worth of everything you could imagine had been delivered to that address. The boss exited the truck and took the package to the door. I was sitting with Donnie in his G-ride listening to the UHF transmission of the boss. A young girl about sixteen answered the door. "Package for Debra Brown. Are you Debra Brown?" says the boss.

"No," says the young girl, "I'll go get her." and she closed the door. The young lady who answered the door had a very deformed face; her jaw and teeth were hideous and she looked a little like a horse.

After the young girl closed he door, the boss said out loud, and to us on the UHF transmitter, and preserved for eternity on the tape recording, "Jesus fucking Christ that girl was fucking ugly. Holy shit! Oh my God, holy shit…!"

Donnie and I were cracking up—we couldn't wait for the boss to take the stand, if this case goes to trial, he is going to be so embarrassed! I guess that's what happens when the boss, who hasn't worked a criminal case in years, gets back in the saddle with the boys for a little undercover work.

* * *

Our plan was to do a controlled delivery of the package at Musigbe's residence. I met with T.J. over at the US Attorney's office and we drafted an affidavit for a search warrant. Federal search warrants are not that easy to get. You have to have specific information that, concealed in the dwelling is, or potentially is, evidence of a violation of a federal statute backed up by solid probable cause. The home is sacred; even a crooks home.

I had good probable cause that Musigbe was committing credit card and bank fraud, and I could have just gotten an arrest warrant, but I wanted to get inside his house and find more evidence. I was sure my investigation was just scratching the surface of a Nigerian fraud ring. I was sure there was more to this than opening bank accounts with counterfeit passports, false identification and kiting checks. The records and documents inside his house could reveal information about a whole gang of Nigerian fraudsters. I always kept Donnie's first rule of fraud cases in mind—"they aren't who they say they are, and it isn't the first time they've done it." If I arrested him, I could have hoped he would give me consent to search his house, but I wasn't counting on that. Nigerians were notorious for not cooperating. I needed a search warrant

The US magistrate signed off on the search warrant, with one exception. The search warrant would not be valid unless and until the package was delivered by US Postal Service employees and Musigbe signed for the package and took it into his home. I got in touch with a Las Vegas postal inspector (PI) and he agreed to help us out by delivering the package. But we had to made sure Musigbe was home for the delivery, so we set up a surveillance of his house.

Early the next morning, Donnie drove the surveillance van over to Musigbe's neighborhood and found a good spot where we could see the front door, the surrounding yard, and the driveway. The Beaver and I stayed put in the back of the van while Donnie got out and walked down the street and around the corner. The boss was waiting and took Donnie back to his G-ride. We hunkered down and waited.

Surveillances can be a kick in the pants, but they can also be boring as hell. Hours and hours of sitting...and waiting...and then the suspect stirs and things get interesting. But in the meantime you sit, and you watch and you wait. It wasn't long before the Beaver and I were bullshitting to pass the time.

The Beaver told me he was thinking about going camping in Colorado and he wanted to know if I knew any good spots where he could pitch a tent and swing in a hammock all afternoon. "Somewhere high up in the mountains," he told me, "where the daytime high isn't over seventy-two degrees." I told him I knew a great spot just south of Aspen, Colorado; it was kind of between Aspen and Crested Butte. That sounded good to him and he wanted to know how I'd found that place.

Back in my Marine Corps days, I was a bombardier/navigator in the A6 Intruder. The A6 was an all-weather attack, close-air-support jet aircraft. The A6 could deliver a nice-size payload of bombs on a target, and to ingress a target we flew at low altitude to evade enemy radar. Consequently, we completed training runs by flying low-level training routes. These routes were published by the FAA, specifically for military low-level training.

I had a good friend in my squadron who was a pilot. He and I were always taking weekend cross-country flights all over the western United States. We both liked to hike, backpack and camp so we'd make notes on remote places we saw as we zipped passed at four hundred and fifty knots, three hundred feet above the ground.

One Friday morning, my buddy Bronco and I were in the squadron ready-room preparing for a weekend cross-country flight to the East Coast. It was one of those CAVU (ceiling and visibility unlimited) September days over the entire United States. Bronco came up with a great idea. "Why don't we fly the VR 1244 (a published military low level training route) through Southern California and Arizona to a bombing range near Yuma, then we could fly at low altitude up through Colorado and land at Buckley AFB in Denver to refuel." Bronco suggested we continue on to the East Coast from Denver and arrive just in time for happy hour at the officers' club. "Outstanding plan," I said to Bronco. "Let's do it!"

We got the charts out and started planning. Thirty minutes later, we had it all worked out—take off IFR (instrument flight rules, meaning we were under positive radar control by the FAA) from Marine Corps Air Station El Toro, cancel the IFR flight plan, enter the low-level training route to Yuma, make two passes at the target and drop our twelve MK-82s (five-hundred-pound high-explosive bombs) to get our required training mission ticked off the board, then fly VFR (visual flight rules, below eighteen thousand feet mean sea level) at low altitude toward Aspen, Colorado; pick up our IFR flight plan when we get over Aspen; and land at Buckley

AFB. I was engrossed in the low level training route flight planning, making sure I had the latitude and longitude correct for each turn point, the outbound headings and I marked the significant terrain features of each turn point on my map, in case our computer system went tits up on us and I had to navigate like a World War II B-17—dead reckoning. The flight profile coming off target at Yuma to Aspen was 150 minutes. "One point five" said Bronco. "We'll have plenty of gas for the low-altitude sightseeing trip trough Colorado!"

So off we went in to the wild blue yonder. Two marines thinking 150 minutes (two and one-half hours) was only one hour and thirty minutes.

The first phase of our plan went off without a hitch. We zipped through the desert of Southern California at 450 knots and two to three hundred feet above the ground. As we approached Silverwood Lake, just west of Big Bear, California, the last turn point before scooting toward the flat Arizona desert and Yuma was the Silverwood Lake dam. We flew low and fast over the water headed directly for the dam. "Did you see those girls?" Bronco asked me. A ski boat was in the lake and off to our left. "I saw a flash of bright orange on the bow," I said. One gal had on a bright orange bikini.

"Let's give them a thrill!" And Bronco executed a perfect knife-edged four-g left-hand turn over the dam, circling back to make another run at the boat. As we completed the 360-degree turn, we disappeared behind the mountains on the west side of the lake. We popped back up over the horizon and commenced a simulated bombing run on the ski boat. Bronco offset our A6 to the right and climbed to twenty-eight hundred feet, rolled inverted; in a left hand climbing turn we visually acquired the target; he snapped it back into a perfect ten-degree dive bombing run, right at the boat.

If you've ever been to a military flight show, you know how frickin' loud a jet aircraft is when it whizzes past you. It is deafening. We were in the ten-degree dive and the ski boat filled our canopy.

We could plainly see three gals, three southern California blondes, tanning themselves with no bikini tops on. Those gals were jumping up and down and waving to us. It was a sight to behold. Though I'm sure their ears rang for hours after that low flyby.

We continued on to the bombing range at Yuma, made two runs at the target, dropping six bombs on each pass. Training mission complete; let's go sightseeing! We climbed to three thousand feet above the ground, slowed to the FAA regulation speed of 250 knots, and settled in for some VFR sightseeing of the Rocky Mountains.

As we headed over the Four Corners into Colorado, I was sitting to the right of Bronco in the cockpit, fat, dumb, and happy with my terrain chart making notes on awesome-looking camping country when I looked over at Bronco. He was tapping the fuel indicator gauge with his finger. Just like you do to your riding lawn mower when you think the gas gauge is broken. I clicked the ICS (inter-cockpit communication system). "What's up? What's the problem?"

"This thing is broken," he tells me. "It says we only have five thousand pounds of jet fuel in the tank."

"Did you transfer the wing tanks to the main?"

"Well yeah," he says. "You think I'm stupid?"

How could that be? Our flight planning indicated we should have seven to eight thousand pounds...it was only one plus thirty coming out of Yuma. "I know," says Bronco. "One hundred and fifty minutes." I think the lightbulb suddenly blinked on bright in our heads at the same time. *Holy shit! One hundred and fifty minutes is two and a half frickin' hours, not one and a half hours. No wonder we're we low on fuel.*

Needless to say our sightseeing trip over Colorado was done. I got out the A6 manual and started doing some serious low fuel flight profile planning. I dialed in Buckley AFB on the navigation and got the distance from our current position. The book said we could make it if we immediately initiated a climb to "Flight Level

God" and pulled the power back to idle and basically glided down hill into Buckley.

I got on the radio with Denver Center and requested an immediate high altitude flight profile with an in-route decent direct into Buckley. Then the dreaded words came back from air traffic control: "Delta Tango One-Five, do you want to declare an emergency?"

I looked at Bronco. Bronco cut in on the radio. *"Negative* emergency, Denver Center; we just need to conserve some fuel."

We got our clearance and Bronco pushed the throttles to MRT (military rated thrust, which is a nice way to say we put the pedal to the medal in order to climb as quickly as possible). We hit our assigned altitude and Denver Center cleared us to descend at our discretion to the initial point for Runway 32 at Buckley. As we glided down to a breathable altitude and it looked like we would actually make it to the end of the runway without flaming out, I looked at Bronco and reminded him that the manual says A6s have been known to flame out with a the fuel indicator gauge reading six hundred pounds—basically saying the old analog gauge was only accurate plus or minus six hundred pounds. He didn't think that was funny.

We landed and taxied to the transient aircraft line to refuel and file our flight plan for the next IFR leg to the East Coast. Once we stopped and the flight line airman chalked the wheels, Bronco went through the engine shutdown procedures. He shut down the number one engine with the throttle and number two engine just up and quit...out of gas.

The Beaver looked at me like I was nuts. He wanted to know if Bronco and I always did dumb stuff. "I thought you were smarter than that?"

I laughed. "Me, too. I learned a very valuable lesson that day."

"What's that?"

"Don't let a pilot do a navigator's flight planning."

We sat there in the back of the surveillance van not saying much for a while, watching Musigbe's house, waiting for some sign he was home.

The Beaver yawned. "Okay Shakespeare, you got any other stories for me? I'm about to fall asleep."

"Hey, did I ever tell you about the time Bronco and I diverted into Malmstrom AFB in Montana?"

The Bronco and I were on one of our infamous weekend cross-countries, zipping around the western US. We were scheduled to land and RON (remain over night) at Mather Air Force Base, near Sacramento, California. Our rule of thumb was, if you planned an RON, be sure it was at an air force base; they had the best bachelor officers' quarters (BOQ) and the best officers' clubs.

We were out just getting instrument flight time that weekend to keep our IFR instrument ratings up to speed. We were at flight level twentysomething, drilling holes in the sky. Half asleep, half bored, but always thinking about a new adventure. Bronco hit the ICS and woke me up. "Ever been to Montana?"

"Not lately," I said.

"Let's divert to Malmstrom and spend the night in Montana… Big sky country!"

"Sure, why not?"

It was late October and when we left El Toro that Friday morning it was seventy-five degrees…neither of us even brought our winter flight jackets with us; we'd submitted our cross-country request to RON at Mather AFB in Sacramento on Friday and RON at Luke AFB, Arizona, on Saturday night, warm weather spots.

We landed at sunset at Malmstrom and we were the only plane on the transient line. It was a beautiful evening. The sunset was awesome with a hint of red clouds and a sky bluer than Vegas. It was breathtaking. We checked into the BOQ and headed to the O Club for a steak and a few beers.

I woke early Saturday morning. The sun was just lighting the eastern horizon. I pulled back the curtains to look out the window and saw a blizzard in the streetlights of the BOQ parking lot. *Holy Shit!* I ran down the hall to Bronco's room and pounded on the door. "Time to go, buddy...the skipper thinks we are in Sacramento and if we get stuck in Montana—well, that ain't good!"

By the time we hightailed it over to base ops the snow had stopped. That was the good news; the bad news was there was eight inches of fresh snow covering the ground. "Yes the airfield is open." the duty officer told us, "but the runway has not been plowed and it won't be until fourteen hundred hours or later." I guess the air force doesn't work on Saturday mornings.

We filed our IFR flight plan—to head south to warmer temperatures and got the weather briefing from the metrological section. Heavy overcast at two thousand feet AGL with the tops at six thousand feet AGL. We had about a sixty-minute window before the next blizzard was scheduled to be rolling in. Winds were out of the southeast at twenty mph, gusting to forty-five mph. *Great! A crosswind on takeoff! What else could go wrong?*

Well, that "what else" was our Intruder covered in snow. I asked the transient line mechanic for a broom and Bronco and I climbed up onto each wing and brushed off as much of the snow as possible. Bronco fired her up and we got clearance to taxi—through eight inches of snow. The air force airmen stood watching us with their mouths agape...crazy marines, crazy, crazy marines.

We roared down that runway with a contrail of snow behind us—it was awesome; we looked like the Blue Angels with their smoke on! Well, maybe not the Blue Angels, but it was pretty cool.

"Speaking of the Blue Angels," I continued, "I was flying with Boots—he was another great pilot in our squadron. We were at the

Chocolate Mountains bombing range out by El Centro, California. The Blue Angels spend the winter months practicing at El Centro Naval Air Station, and as Boots and I were cruising around the desert at about three hundred feet AGL and four hundred knots—*whoosh!* Two of those Blue Angel bastards buzzed us. Passed us on our left, about fifty feet below and seventy-five to eighty knots faster. After they passed us they pulled up into the vertical and did a victory roll…Show-offs."

I was getting ready to tell him about the time Bronco and I almost hit the side of a vertical canyon wall when Musigbe showed himself. He walked out to his car, retrieved something, and walked back in the house. It was time for the mailman. The postal inspector drove up in a white mail delivery truck, the ones with the driver's side on the right and walked up to the door. The PI did a great job of engaging Musigbe in conversation, on tape of course, about the package from Lagos.

"Oh yeah, I've been waiting for this. It's from my brother in Nigeria," he said.

"Great!" replied the postal inspector. "Thanks and have a good day."

We waited a few minutes for the PI to clear the area and I made the call to execute the warrant. And in we went. Musigbe was a little surprised to find himself in handcuffs. We searched the house and recovered numerous false and counterfeit drivers' licenses, and blank checks from various banks in Atlanta, Houston, and Las Vegas, along with a few MasterCard and Visa credit cards.

Unfortunately, every one of the counterfeit identifications had his picture, so I was not into a gang of Nigerians as I'd hoped, but at least the names on the counterfeit driver's licenses and passports from Nigeria matched. He claimed his real name was John Alitio. In keeping with the grand tradition of the Nigerian fraudster, he didn't know anything and wanted to speak to an attorney. Probably a smart move. US Immigration discovered he'd entered the United States on a student visa and, once again, decided to stay. *Great system, those student visas, really great system.*

I've arrested numerous Nigerians over the years, and not one of them has ever taken the case to trial. And this guy was no different, he pleaded guilty, but not before creating quite a scene in the US district court at sentencing. Musigbe/Alitio got on his hands and knees before the Judge and begged for mercy. He had his hands clasped before him and tears streaming down his cheeks, as the US district court judge ordered him to prison to be followed by deportation back to his homeland.

Chapter 11

The Boston Patriot

Las Vegas is a gambling town. The Redhead and I were not really into gambling. As a matter of fact, the Redhead hated casinos. She hated the Strip. She hated the hot, windy desert. She hated Vegas. She missed her beach and her cool ocean breezes. For my next assignment I still had my sights on PPD in Washington, DC; hot, muggy Washington, DC…Boy, is she going to love that climate!

Sometime during my tour of duty in Las Vegas, the state of California started a lottery. Buying a ticket cost one dollar and you had a chance to win a million-dollar jackpot. It was big news in Las Vegas. All the TV stations and the newspaper were decrying the lotto as the end to casino gambling in Vegas. It was doom and gloom…they declared tourists wouldn't come to Las Vegas to gamble if they could play the lotto right at home! *Really?* Really. I used to just shake my head at the stupidity of the local news anchors and reporters, sensationalizing everything.

One night we were watching the local newscast and they had another doom-and-gloom report on how the California lottery was going to kill Las Vegas tourism. Not a report on how the California lottery might, maybe, adversely affect tourism; nope! Tourism was as good as dead in Vegas.

One of the blonde talking heads was reporting from the field in a small town off of I-15 just across the California state line with Nevada. This was a one-horse desert town with nothing there except a small gas station quick stop—a "stop and rob," as the Beaver used to call them. People were lined up in the hot desert sun for over a mile, waiting to buy a California lottery ticket. It was proof. Visual proof, Vegas was going to take its last breath any day now. Call an undertaker!

After her breathless report on the sad situation, the reporter cut to an interview with a major casino's bookmaker. This was the guy who set the odds at the sports book. He was the guru of gambling...he was *the* authority. Blondie interviews the bookmaker; he is sitting at a cluttered desk and the camera angle is from the side and a looking down at him. He looks to be in his sixties, and his crown, indicating male-pattern baldness, shines brightly in the television lights. He has a stogie between his teeth that he politely takes out of his mouth before answering the interviewer's questions. He is lambasting the ignorant fools for buying lottery tickets.

"It's a sucker bet," he says. "Your odds are much better at the craps table, the blackjack table, heck, even in the sports book, your odds of winning in Vegas are much, much better than buying a lottery ticket. You like to play the numbers? Come to Vegas, that's exactly what Keno is—you pick the numbers. And with Keno, you get many, many choices of combinations to complete a winning

Keno card. With that scam of a California lottery, you have to pick six, for Pete's sake. It's a sucker bet!"

Blondie smiles. Oh yeah, she's just confirmed for all Las Vegans that standing in line to buy a lottery ticket is a waste of time—get down to the local casino, hit the tables. One last question for Mr. Bookmaker. "Would you buy a dollar California lottery ticket?"

He looks straight at her and with out missing a beat says, "For a buck? Heck, yeah! It's worth a buck."

I still laugh about that interview when I think about it. Uh, and guess what? Been to Vegas lately? It's still hopping and it always will be, because it's Vegas, baby…it's Vegas.

My old SAIC was right about one thing—gambling has ruined many a man. Las Vegas was full of folks who would spend their last dime on a bet and then rob the kid's piggy bank for one more bet, just one more. They'd also rob a real bank…with or without a gun.

One of the things I learned early on at the LAFO working check forgery cases was that the sweetest, nicest little old lady, one who wouldn't even think about shoplifting a pack of gum from the neighborhood 7-Eleven, would cash a government check without blinking an eye. It's what I called the Great Depression syndrome. The government's got plenty of money; it's mine for the taking. The husband's dead? Been dead for years, but the bumbling idiots in the bureaucracy of the Social Security Administration (SSA) keeps mailing those monthly checks to Grandpa Jones. And Grandma Jones keeps signing his name and depositing them in her account.

Inevitably, Grandma would claim she notified the SSA…twice, that the old man was *dead*. But the checks keep coming, so Grandma keeps cashing them. They didn't think they were stealing money, they thought the government was giving them money. That's what Mr. Roosevelt did right? He gave you money.

What they didn't realize was the government doesn't lose money on anything. When the bureaucracy catches up with the paperwork, they take it back from you...or at least, they take it back from your bank. And the next thing you know, Grandma Jones owes First National Bank forty grand.

The Redhead had a quite a few collateral duties at her small Las Vegas bank. One of those duties was loss prevention. She told me about a bank employee they suspected was embezzling money. And when confronted, she lied about it. They always lie. They always minimize. "I was gonna redeposit the money, I just needed to make my mortgage payment this month!" But when the bank dug deeper, they found thousands of dollars, ten's of thousands of dollars missing. Why? Because she was addicted to gambling.

I wanted to work that case in the worst way, mainly because I wanted to work any case I could, but there was no credit card fraud in this one, just plain old embezzlement. So I reluctantly had to tell the Redhead to call my friends over at Freddie, Bernie, and Irving. Embezzlement, that's right up their alley. Besides, I had more than enough fraud cases to work.

Years later, toward the end of my career, I was sent to the one-man office of the Anchorage, Alaska, RA for a thirty-day temporary assignment. I got a telephone call from a local hospital administrator. She told me one of their bookkeepers was using a hospital MasterCard to get cash advances. I opened an investigation and uncovered one $120,000 worth of fraudulent transactions by the bookkeeper. This was also embezzlement, but it was credit card fraud—my criminal jurisdiction.

I was digging into the suspect's background and obtaining the evidence I needed to arrest her when the hospital administrator called the office. She wanted to drop the charges, the bookkeeper wrote the hospital a check for $120,000 and paid them back. *Are you kidding me?* I told her I had two problems with this: first, the federal system does not require a victim to press charges like local judicial systems, and secondly how many people do you know who have $120,000 in their checking account? "Oh!" she said. "I guess you are right."

Sure enough, as I got further into the investigation I found two previous employers from whom she had embezzled for close to two hundred grand. Both employers fired her and did not file a police report. I was shocked! But I'm a law and order guy and I just can't imagine not calling the police on something like that. You have to remember the Donnie's undeniable fact of fraudsters: "It's not the first time they've done it and they are not who they say they are."

* * *

We worked very closely with the bank loss prevention guys, and some of them were really good about putting a solid case together before they called us. I loved those; they were easy arrests, easy cases to work to the finish line. I was just the anchor leg in the mile relay. I just had to complete the last lap.

Stan Fleck was one of those investigators at Valley Bank in Las Vegas. He'd been in the loss prevention, fraud business a long time and he always brought us a nice, neat package of an investigation... when Sally, our administrative aide said Stan was on line two; Donnie, the Beaver and me would climb all over each other to get to line two. And on that day I won the race to the telephone.

Stan told me he was working a credit card fraud case that was a thirteen-hundred-dollar loss to Valley Bank. He had three Valley Bank MasterCards issued to three different people and the actual people whose name was used to open the accounts had not applied for the credit cards. Two were employees of America West Airlines and the other was an employee of the Nevada Department of Transportation. Identity theft before identity theft was a buzzword.

Stan found that all three credit cards had the same address. The address was a commercial mail drop business, one of those places you could rent a mailbox and buy a greeting card or have your Christmas packages sent out via UPS. A legitimate business, but a haven for fraudsters. I would venture to say of all the credit card cases I investigated, the suspect was using a commercial mail drop as his address 75 percent of the time.

Stan had contacted the mail drop and found the address was listed as the "America West Employees Anniversary Committee, Chuck Wright, chairman." Stan was handing me the baton and all I had to do was run the final lap.

The Beaver and I went to the real address of the Nevada Department of Transportation employee to see if he had any insight into who was using his identity to open credit card accounts. Mr. Pontsler was more than willing to help, and he had some good information. Right off the bat, he suspected a fellow office worker at the department named Ingrid.

"Do you know where she lives?" I asked him.

"No," he said. "No idea where she lives, but I've heard her say her roommate is a flight attendant with America West Airlines." Thank you, Mr. Pontsler. And good luck cleaning up your credit report, because it's going to be a nightmare.

I made a telephone call to the America West Airlines security manager and he was able to dig around a little for me. He called back a few days later and said the airlines had recently terminated a flight attendant, and her coworkers remembered she lived with a roommate named Ingrid. The former employee was Roberta Bellefontaine.

Stan checked in with me a few days later and reported he'd found that one of the credit cards had been used as a reference at a Las Vegas furniture store to open a line of credit.

I got a photo of Roberta from America West and put together a photo spread and headed over to the furniture store. I walked the store manager through the transaction. I always liked to do this with a witness to get them thinking about the event; it helps them remember details about the incident you are investigating. "Oh yeah, I remember that purchase," he told me, "The woman's name was Eugenia something. She was a talker, and she said she worked as a flight attendant for an airline."

"Do you recognize Eugenia in any of these six pictures?" I asked.

"Oh yeah," he said, "Number four, that's her...I remember that name Eugenia; never heard that name before and she said she was a flight attendant. You don't run into those everyday...interesting job, flight attendant."

The Beaver and I found Bellefontaine at the address listed for her in the telephone book. Ingrid had unfortunately been fired from the Department of Transportation, and according to Roberta, she'd left Las Vegas for parts unknown. It was just as well because T.J. declined to prosecute Ingrid as part of the conspiracy—the evidence against her was too thin.

Roberta was a nice young lady with a serious gambling problem. She was very cooperative and gave a full written confession to applying for and receiving twenty-four different credit cards in the names of various America West employees and one Nevada Department of Transportation employee. This gal would have never even thought about robbing a bank, but she didn't even think twice about stealing from an entity like a bank. *A bank? The government? What's the difference, it is a victimless crime, right?* Tell Mr. Pontsler and those twenty-three other real people who just had their credit ruined that it is a victimless crime. I don't think they'd agree.

* * *

I wish all cases were that simple and quick. Some were, but most weren't. Especially the Boston Patriot investigation; he was a tough nut to crack.

I think just about every federal law enforcement agency in New England was after the Boston Patriot. He was a prolific fraudster; he was full-time and made his living off of credit card fraud. Either that, or he was working for a large criminal enterprise and he was just a small cog in the wheel. Either way, the Boston Patriot was into several East Coast banks for hundreds of thousands of dollars in losses. It was only a matter of time before he came to Las Vegas...at some point, all criminals come to Las Vegas, either to spend their ill-gotten goods or to continue the scam.

In the eighties and nineties obtaining a cash advance at a casino involved a paper check called a Comchek. The system was very common in roadside truck stops as a way for a traveling truck driver to get cash from his trucking line while he was on the road. There were various ways for the employer to get the cash to Comchek, just as with Western Union. But at a casino, the customer used a Comchek machine that was sort of like an ATM. The customer would insert their credit card, select an amount, and then go to the casino cage to get the check. The customer would present the credit card and his identification to the cashier, who would retrieve the printed Comchek from the printer, and have the customer endorse the back. It was a great system, because it created a nice paper trail and all paper trails will lead you to a suspect.

Postal inspectors investigating the Boston Patriot's crimes gave him his moniker. He was an unknown suspect. He was using newly issued Bank of Boston credit cards stolen from the mail before they reached the mailboxes of the true cardholder. And he was using counterfeit Massachusetts and Rhode Island driver's licenses as identification for cash advances at New England banks. Postal inspectors in Boston had obtained bank surveillance photos of him standing at teller windows getting cash advances. The early photos showed a white male with dark hair and glasses wearing a white New England Patriots football jersey...it seemed he was always wearing the New England Patriots jersey…and thus, the Boston Patriot was born.

The three of us worked with the Comchek security department all the time on various credit card fraud cases in Las Vegas. All those Nigerians getting cash advances at the casinos were cashing Comcheks to get their money. One day I was on the telephone with an investigator from Comchek, discussing an arrest I'd made on a Nigerian. As we wrapped up our conversation, he casually mentioned he had a fraud case involving twenty-seven Comcheks cashed at Las Vegas casinos on the same day. He said nineteen different credit cards had been used to fraudulently obtain the cash advances at nineteen different casinos. He told me he'd been unsuccessful with tying these cash advances to a known suspect, "Would you be interested in taking a look at them?"

"Sure," I said. "Send them to me and I'll see if I can come up with something."

When I got the original Comcheks I took a good look at them. The fronts of the checks were automatically filled in by the check printer machine, with the name of the individual cardholder and the credit card account number used for the transaction and a time/date stamp the check was printed. The backs of each check were endorsed by the cardholder, and all casino cage cashiers who completed the transactions wrote the cardholder's identification number and state in the blank spaces provided on the check. Each check also had a time/date stamp on the back, indicating the casino name, date, and time it was cashed.

Multiple Rhode Island driver's licenses had been used as identification for the cash advances; I ran each driver's license number through the National Law Enforcement Telecommunications System, and each driver's license number proved to be fictitious. The nineteen credit cards were all Bank of Boston MasterCards, and an investigator from Bank of Boston told me each card was issued by Bank of Boston and bank records indicated they were mailed to the true cardholders. All nineteen true cardholders reported they did not receive the MasterCards in the mail.

The Boston Patriot had finally hit Las Vegas.

I noticed a very interesting pattern. On July 25 the first two transactions were at Bally's Casino, followed by one across Flamingo Road, at Maxim's Casino. Then at the corner of Flamingo Road and Las Vegas Boulevard the suspect hit the Flamingo Hilton for two transactions of twenty-four hundred dollars apiece. Just north on the strip his next stop was the Holiday Casino, then the Sands Casino, and the Riviera Casino. Each of these cash advances was for twenty-four hundred dollars and all on the same credit card. The next two Comcheks were cashed at the Sahara Casino on Las Vegas Boulevard. Both cash advances were for twenty-four hundred dollars on the same credit card account. The suspect then crossed Las Vegas Boulevard and hit the Stardust Casino for two twenty-four-hundred-dollar cash advances and continued back south on the strip to Caesar's Palace. And he was right back to the corner of Flamingo Road and Las Vegas Boulevard. The time and date stamps on the Comcheks showed he had time to walk from one casino to the next. He made a nice loop, from Flamingo Road north on the strip to Sahara Road and turned back south to Flamingo Road.

The next date time stamp was at the Palace Station, off the strip on Sahara Road west of I-15. Then the Vegas World back on the strip north of Sahara Road. Downtown to Glitter Gulch and Fremont Street, where he hit the Golden Nugget. Across Fremont Street to Binion's Horseshoe, the Union Plaza, over to the Vegas Club, then the California Club.

Then he hit the strip again, the Maxim, the Marina Casino at Tropicana and Las Vegas Boulevard. He finished up at the Stardust one final time. Jesus fucking Christ. Sixty-four thousand dollars in cash advances in one night, in less than eight hours. Not a bad day working at the Fraud Mine. He was raking in the cash at an eight-thousand-dollar-per-hour pace.

No doubt the Boston Patriot was in Vegas. Now I just needed to identify this unknown suspect and get him in custody.

I packaged the original Comcheks up and sent them off to the Secret Service Forensic Lab in Washington, DC, with two requests. First, I requested a handwriting examination to see if the same unknown person authored the endorsements on the backs of all twenty-seven Comcheks; secondly, I requested a fingerprint/palm print examination to see if this unknown suspect had fingerprints on file with my buddies at the FBI.

It took a few weeks, but I finally got the handwriting analysis back from the lab. The Secret Service handwriting examiner concluded that the same, unknown hand authored all twenty-seven signatures. Beautiful. Now I knew it was one guy and one guy only. I'm not after a gang; I'm after one guy. The MO was definitely the Boston Patriot. The handwriting report stated that a review of known Secret Service handwriting specimens revealed the author was not of record with the Secret Service.

For aeons Secret Service agents have routinely obtained handwriting examples from suspects. It was part of our investigative protocol, going way back to US Treasury check investigations since Uncle Sugar started issuing paper checks and Secret Service agents started investigating forgery of those checks. We continued that protocol with our fraud investigations. Always get a handwriting sample from the suspect or defendant. It might come in handy someday to another agent. But this guy was not of record, so chances were a Secret Service agent had never interviewed him.

Now I had to wait for the fingerprint examination and it was worth the wait. The Secret Service lab positively identified Edward Capone's fingerprints on all twenty-seven Comcheks. Who the hell is Edward Capone? And where is he?

I briefed T.J. on the case and he told me to write up an affidavit for an arrest warrant. "Let's get a warrant in the system in case he gets stopped by the police somewhere. Then we can get him extradited to Las Vegas and bring him to justice." His last known address was in Providence, Rhode Island. I contacted the postal inspectors in Boston and sent a request to the Secret Service offices in New England to attempt to locate and arrest Capone.

I did a utility search for Clark County Nevada and I'll be damned if he didn't live right in Las Vegas. Or at least someone with the same name and social security number did. The Beaver and I set out to try and positively identify Capone. As the Beaver drove us out toward his residence I was trying to come up with a good surveillance plan to watch him for a positive identification. As normal for the Las Vegas RA, all three of us were very busy and a long drawn out surveillance this week wasn't going to work. The Beaver told me to not make this so damn complicated. We know what he looks like, we've got good photos of him…let's knock on his door and if that's him we'll arrest him.

Sometimes simplicity is the best road to take. It was mid-morning and we rang the doorbell. Edward Capone, in his boxers and white tank top T-shirt answered the door. "Edward Capone? Secret Service," I said as I began to identify myself. Capone's eyes got real big and he retreated backward into the small apartment living room. He was just out of my reach and I couldn't grab ahold of him. The Beaver and I were dressed in our normal casual attire and we both had our gold US Secret Service badges hanging from our necks by chains. I had my Secret Service credentials in my left hand, the Beaver and I quickly stepped through the threshold into the living room.

The space between the front door and the back of a couch in the living room was about three paces; Capone was stepping back, retreating…I got the impression he thought we were a couple of wise guys sent to break his legs, I started yelling, "Police, police!" and the Beaver moved quickly toward Capone to grab him before he could get to a weapon. In the next split second, all five foot eight and three hundred pounds of Capone fell backward over the couch and the Beaver fell forward on top of him.

He sat handcuffed on an easy chair and asked if he could get dressed before he met the judge. "Sure," I said, "Which way is the bedroom?" I grabbed a pair of sweat pants off the bedroom floor and how about a shirt? He needs a shirt. I looked in his closet and found the white New England Patriots football jersey. Perfect. The Boston Patriot was in custody.

The Beaver and I took Capone to the US magistrate for his initial appearance. As the judge entered the courtroom and took the bench, Edward Capone collapsed out of his chair and sprawled on the floor. The two courtroom US Marshals rushed to his side. My suspicions that he was tied to organized crime increased dramatically. Mobsters always passed out on the courtroom floor. *Why do they do this?* I don't know, it must be in the mobster handbook…

Donnie arrested a made guy once, an old Chicago guy left over from the Spilotro years. What's the first thing he did in the courtroom? Fainted. "Call an ambulance," his lawyer screamed. I tell you, they always do that or something very similar. The Beaver once arrested another old Chicago guy for counterfeiting. This old mobster only had one leg, but walked around with the aid of a prosthetic. We had been following this guy around Las Vegas for weeks, and if you didn't know he was missing one leg, you would never know it by watching him walk. He barely had a limp. The Beaver indicted him and contacted his attorney to arrange for a voluntary surrender to the Secret Service. On the agreed upon surrender day, the old mobster showed up in a wheelchair, without his prosthetic leg.

It is always something with these guys, trying to play the sympathy card with the court, I guess.

Of course, Capone was okay and ready to proceed, but not without his attorney scolding the government for arresting his client at his home—bursting in, disturbing the neighbors and the quiet serenity of everyone's mid-morning coffee. Mr. Capone would have gladly turned himself in but these two thugs from the Secret Service barged into his home *and* the government refused to bring the defendant's prescription medicine along to the US Marshals lockup. Of course, Capone didn't say shit about needing prescription medication when we led him out of his apartment in handcuffs; the only thing wrong with Capone was his crime spree was over and he knew it.

As the court proceeding got under way, the judge reviewed the financial statement of the defendant. He qualified for a public defender, but yet, one of Vegas's most expensive defense attorneys was sitting at the defense table.

After his arrest I sent notifications to all the New England area Secret Service Offices, hoping one of them could get their US attorney to prosecute him for the crimes in their jurisdictions. But unfortunately no US attorney on the East Coast was aggressive enough to take the case. And I guess you can't really blame them. Why take up court time for a defendant who is in prison? The Boston Patriot pleaded guilty to my indictment and only served eighteen months in the federal penitentiary followed by three years' probation.

Chapter 12

Leroy's Race and Sports Book

The Food Stamp Act of 1964, administered by the US Department of Agriculture, was enacted to ensure "No American Goes Hungry." The actual "coupons" or "stamps" are printed by the US Treasury and are thus an obligation of the United States, and counterfeiting a food stamp is the same as counterfeiting a Federal Reserve note. Believe it or not, the US Secret Service investigates food stamp fraud. Nowadays printed food stamps are obsolete and have been replaced with debit cards. But back in the eighties when I was in Las Vegas, your uncle Sugar was giving out paper food stamps, actually called food coupons. We didn't work many food stamp cases; as a matter fact, in L.A. I don't remember ever working one. But Las Vegas was a different situation.

The US Department of Agriculture (USDA) Office of Inspector General (IG) also investigated food stamp fraud. The USDA IG's regional office in Sacramento had jurisdiction over the state of Nevada, and one day they paid a visit to our office in Las Vegas. The Agriculture IG had received numerous complaints from citizens that stores and shops in Las Vegas were committing food stamp fraud by accepting food stamps for goods and items other than food. So the USDA IG had decided it was time to do a little food stamp enforcement in the Las Vegas area.

They wanted to put together a small task force of IG agents and Secret Service agents to investigate the suspected fraud. It sounded like a great idea and I volunteered to be the Secret Service case agent. And, boy, did I get my hands full with this one! Never volunteer.

As the three of us sat in the boss's office and he explained the proposed taskforce, I couldn't figure out why Donnie and the Beaver were sitting on their hands. I was squirming left and right and falling all over myself to get the boss to assign the case agent duties to me. They were sitting on their hands because both those guys are a lot smarter than me.

The USDA IG case agent and I went over to see T.J. at the US Attorney's office. If the US Attorney was not all in on this one, that is, if he wouldn't agree to prosecute the suspects we wanted to turn into defendants, we would be wasting our time. And that's probably why we didn't work food stamp fraud cases in L.A. The US Attorney's office in Los Angeles, like most cities across the nation, had dollar thresholds for prosecution—they only wanted to touch the big-time crooks. But not T.J. "I'll prosecute any case you bring me, boys. Go get them."

And so we did…

There is a tremendous amount of paperwork that goes into an investigation, and if you throw in some undercover work with consensual intercepts, the paperwork gets pretty heavy. It wasn't long before I realized Donnie and the Beaver knew what they were doing when they wanted no part of this operation. Jesus Christ! Suddenly, I was swamped.

Each time an agent uses a tape recorder or the UHF transmitter, or uses the telephone to record a conversation with a crook, reports and requests have to be submitted to headquarters *before* you use the equipment. In an emergency, an agent can get verbal approval from headquarters to intercept a suspect, but that was the exception and not the rule. If an agent doesn't have the proper authorizations in place, a defense attorney can get the entire recorded evidence declared inadmissible, and then your case is shot.

The USDA had a long list of tips from ordinary citizens on merchants who were suspected of abusing the food stamp system, and we set out to see if any of the tips were worth investigating. The USDA case agent was Special Agent Paul Broxterman. And he was an outstanding undercover agent. He was a skinny kid with a scraggly beard. One of those beards that was splotchy with a little hair here and a little hair there. And when he pulled on his blue jeans and cowboy boots, he was the last guy you thought was a cop. He was good, very good.

Paul and I spent about three months working these food stamp cases and we became close friends. I think the Beaver was a little jealous. I didn't have time for cheeseburgers with the Beaver for a long time. I didn't have time to hit the gym in the mornings with the guys; I didn't have time for a beer on Friday nights with them. I was one busy little agent. Paul and I were about to arrest thirty-five defendants, but first we had to build the case.

To work these food stamp fraud investigations we had to wire up Paul with the UHF transmitter and a tape recorder. We didn't have a snitch, so we had to hit these merchants cold to see if the complaint was true—that they were accepting food stamps for items other than food. We weren't out to entrap any merchants: either they were abusing the system or they weren't. Paul would go into one of the stores reported to the USDA and try to buy cigarettes or other nonfood items, or redeem the stamps for cash. If the merchant didn't bite and Paul was turned down we'd close the case against that particular merchant as unsubstantiated, and move on to the next one.

One of the citizen complaints the USDA received was that people were buying and selling food stamps right on the sidewalk outside the welfare office in North Las Vegas. Paul would wire up, take a pocket full of marked USDA control food stamps and sit on a bench outside the welfare office. Holy crap, business was good! I could not believe how many folks would stop and asked this scraggly bearded bum if he had any food stamps for sale or if he wanted to buy some food stamps. Our ultimate goal was to find an organized ring that was dealing in illegal food stamps; we didn't necessarily want to arrest some poor guy just trying to pad his pantry to feed his kids— that was never our intention. But to get Paul into a criminal ring, he had to see who was buying and who was selling. Like I've said, I'm always been amazed at how many people, otherwise honest citizens, wouldn't think twice about cheating their uncle Sugar.

Paul had a few repeat customers and we started to focus in on these guys—maybe they were part of a ring. Paul was a good actor and he could talk the talk and walk the walk. One guy kept showing up to buy food stamps from Paul, but he'd only pay twenty-five cents on the dollar. The going rate was fifty cents; this guy was obviously a good target. We figured he must be reselling the food stamps to make a profit, so we started a surveillance of him. He was an older gentleman named Harold, who looked like an old Vegas gambler if there ever was one. Skinny as a rail with gray, ash-colored skin. A cigarette dangled from his lips at all times and he squinted when he talked to you, trying to keep the smoke out of his eyes. He smelled of whiskey most days. He was so skinny there was no way he was using food stamps to feed himself. He was obviously on the Vegas diet of nicotine and alcohol. As I watched him through my binoculars I thought to myself, *He looks like a cigarette, with his close-cropped gray hair as the ash hanging off the end!*

Harold spent a lot of time at a downtown joint called Leroy's Race and Sports Book. Leroy's was an old Vegas bookmaking place on Main Street between the Greyhound bus station and the Union Plaza Hotel and Casino. It was a real Vegas dive with a lot of old-time sports book characters. Leroy's was the kind of place with the high back wall with racetrack and professional sports odds handwritten in grease pencil; no fancy electronic red and yellow odds lines posted here, no sir! Good old-fashioned handwriting.

One day Harold sat down next to Paul on the bench outside the welfare office and they struck up a conversation. He must have had one too many Old Crows that day, because he was in a talkative mood. Paul asked Harold if he knew where he could unload a large quantity of food stamps. Paul said he had access to large quantities of stolen food stamps and he needed to make a big score and get out of town. This nickel and dime action on the sidewalk was too slow.

"Sure, Paulie," said Harold. "Come on down to Leroy's, the bartenders will buy all you can get and they will pay you fifty cents on the dollar." Thank God! We finally got some decent info on a ring. Sitting in the back of the surveillance van on those hot Vegas afternoons watching Paul sell food stamps to the Vegas downtrodden was getting old.

The next morning about ten o'clock we wired up Paul and sent him in. The Golden Nugget parking garage had a nice view of Leroy's front door and when I parked on the top level, I had a bird's-eye view of the front and part of the side alley.

Paul would spend a few hours every day in Leroy's getting to know the employees and the regulars who were propped up at the bar. We had Paul go in at various hours during the day. He always carried a couple of food stamp booklets in his pocket: marked USDA food stamp coupons. The coupons were marked so if he did succeed at selling some food stamps we could trace where they were redeemed.

Paul would sit at the bar nursing a Bud Light for hours, talking the talk. He would put his hand over his mouth, speaking into the microphone taped to his chest and give me a running narrative of his observations. He noticed the two bartenders were openly buying food stamps from patrons. They'd make a buy and slip the booklets under a towel on the counter along the back wall.

Paul was developing a relationship with Dale and Rich, the two bartenders at Leroy's, but he wasn't getting the feeling the time was right to offer to sell some food stamps. He didn't want to blow this opportunity because if they declined his offer we'd have to shut it down and move on. Finally, one morning Harold walked in and sat next to "Paulie." Paul bought him a shot of Old Crow, with a PBR chaser...the Breakfast of Champions.

Harold provided the opening we needed...the snitch we didn't have. "Hey, Dale, my buddy Paulie here is the guy you need to talk to. He's a stand-up guy and he can help you out." That was all Paul needed, a good introduction and he was off to the races. Paul started small, one booklet for fifty cents on the dollar. A couple of days later another one. Then Dale introduced Paulie to Rich, the afternoon-shift bartender. A booklet here, a booklet there. *But what are they doing with these food stamps?*

One day Paul noticed a waitress from another establishment came in the side door off the alley and talked to Dale at the end of the bar. Dale was carrying the towel he'd picked up off the back counter of the bar. As they conversed a little, Paul was narrating to me the play by play. "Looks like she's changing a twenty for smaller bills," he whispered into his hand, "Dale gave her change and put the towel on her serving tray." I grabbed the binoculars and watched her walk out the side door and continue down the alley. She turned right at a corner in the alley and disappeared from my sight. The only business or building to the right of the alley was the Golden Gate Casino. Paul said the waitress was in her mid-fifties with a really bad blonde wig. She was either a cocktail waitress or a Keno runner at the Golden Gate Casino. The Beaver left his surveillance position and walked over to the Golden Gate. He came out about thirty minutes later and said, "Shit! All the cocktail waitresses and Keno runners look like they're in their mid-fifties and half of them have blonde wigs."

The next afternoon Paul and I went gambling at the Golden Gate. We sat apart at the main bar and played video poker. Of course, we sipped a beer; you have to blend in for Pete's sake. Paul narrowed our search down to two waitresses running drinks to the slot machine patrons. Jan and Evelyn; Evelyn or Jan. One of those was our girl.

A few days later Paul was back at Leroy's selling food stamps to Rich. At this point in the investigation we had successfully identified nine players in Leroy's selling food stamps to Dale and Rich. In order to get a good prosecutable hand-to-hand fraudulent transaction, Paul would approach one of the nine when he saw them in Leroy's and he would offer to buy or sell food stamps from them. Paul knew all nine by their first names and we had gotten some good surveillance photos of each of them as they left the bar. With Paul's eyewitness testimony and the hand-to-hand exchange of money with Paul, that's all T.J. needed to prove conspiracy. They were as good as arrested.

Now we needed to identify the waitress and see what she was doing with the food stamps. Paul grabbed a spot at the bar closer to the alley side door and sure enough the waitress came in to get "change" from Rich. Jan…it was Jan. We had a surveillance team in the Golden Gate to see if they could figure out what she was doing with the food stamp booklets once she got back to work.

The Beaver reported that when Jan walked into the Golden Gate after her "change run" to Leroy's she didn't have a towel on her serving tray. Now, the next big mystery…what the fuck did she do with the food stamp booklets? We tried every angle possible to get a good surveillance position to see that entire alleyway, but it was too narrow and had two many angles—it wasn't a straight shot from Leroy's side door to the Golden Gate back entrance. Later on we even had an ATF agent help us by sitting at the bar in Leroy's with Paul to follow Jan out the side door, though that never worked out. We speculated she was dumping those booklets somewhere or giving them to someone in that alley.

One day a regular named Jimmy, who'd we'd identified as selling food stamps to Dale, asked Paul if he would be willing to buy a booklet at fifty cents on the dollar. Why not? The more hand-to-hand illegal transactions, the better and it would add an additional count in the indictment against Jimmy. Paul said, "Sure, but let's go outside." They went out the side door to the front part of the alley where we could watch the transaction, get some photos of Paul exchanging money with the guy, and back him up in case Jimmy had a little armed robbery in mind.

About the time they were ready to exchange the cash, Jan walked by Paul and into Leroy's. Paul bought the food stamps from Jimmy and then offered him a smoke. They stood in the alley smoking a cigarette and bullshitting about horse race betting. Jimmy was an "expert" at playing the horses and he didn't mind giving his new buddy some handicap pointers. Jan eventually walked out the side door, right past Paul. Paul said good-bye to Jimmy and followed Jan at a safe distance. As he rounded the ninety-degree turn near the end of the alley, he plainly saw Jan hand the white towel to a white male, about thirty years old. His name was Bobby and he would be defendant number thirty-five.

It was time to wrap up this task force. We had thirty-five suspects, total; thirteen were from Leroy's, twenty were repeat customers from the sidewalk in front of the Welfare Office, and two dirty store clerks working at one of the food stores. T.J. and I began presenting the cases to a federal grand jury about three weeks before we finished up at Leroy's, and we were saving all the arrest warrants for one big roundup. T.J. wanted to make one big splash in the local news. "It's not going to stop food stamp fraud in Las Vegas," he told me, "but it'll sure slow it down for a few months."

The conspiracy indictment for the Leroy's Race and Sports Book suspects was our last case, and once the grand jury came back with a True Bill (a majority vote by the members of the grand jury that probable cause existed for the suspects to face trial) we started putting together an arrest plan for each suspect and assigned individual teams to each. The idea was to arrest all thirty-five, or as many as we could find in one day. USDA brought in five agents from Sacramento, the LAFO sent six guys to Las Vegas to assist. I had all the ATF guys, DEA guys, US Marshals, a few LVMPD detectives and Gaming Control agents for Leroy's. Freddie, Bernie, and Irving chose not to participate—or maybe inviting them slipped my mind; either way, we had plenty of help. Now we just needed to find all of suspects.

On takedown day we briefed the arrest teams early in the morning at our office. Donnie and the Beaver put together an arrest packet for each defendant with photos, criminal history printouts, driver's license printouts, and all the information we had on their residences and hangouts. Some even had jobs, so we included employment information.

At six that morning the arrest teams dispersed throughout Las Vegas and started hauling suspects into the office. By eleven we had eighteen to twenty in custody, all sitting handcuffed in chairs in our hallway. The place looked like the Clark County Jail intake center. It was awesome! Our plan was to have Paul go to Leroy's about one in the afternoon and he would call me when enough of the players showed up. Dale and Rich did a shift change at two in the afternoon, so we had planned to at least wait until Rich showed up for his shift. The rest would be rounded up later that afternoon.

Paul was antsy. He wanted to go to Leroy's a little before noon. "What the heck," I told him, "Go ahead, I'll expect a call about two."

Paul wasn't in Leroy's ten minutes when the office telephone rang. It was Paul on the pay phone from Leroy's. He was breathless, "Get down here now...right now! Bring all the arrest teams, they are all here!"

"What do you mean they're all there"? I ask.

"I mean all thirteen of them are in Leroy's right now!" he said. "Rich is in here in his civvies sitting right next to me at the bar. Bobby, Jimmy, Harold...all of 'em!" I could picture Paul on the pay phone in the back by the restrooms surveying the patrons at Leroy's.

My buddy Vinnie G. from the Gaming Control Board and I walked in first. We all had on raid jackets and plenty of uniformed cops. The joint went quiet, real quiet. Vinnie G. and I made a beeline for the owner's office. He was more than happy to cooperate with the Gaming Control Board. "Of course you can search my establishment if you would like to," he told Vinnie. I had him execute a written consent to search form for me waiving his Fourth Amendment rights. The agents and cops started hooking up people left and right. You could have heard a pin drop in Leroy's. Every single person sitting at the bar, most of them suspects, just stared straight ahead. You could tell they were just trying to disappear.

I overheard the Beaver talking to a guy at the bar as I walked past. "Nope that ain't me," he lied. The Beaver held up a photo of our suspect adjacent to his face. "Yep that's you, Bobby," said the Beaver. "Stand up and turn around."

Word was spreading fast through downtown; the feds are taking down Leroy's. Of course, no one knew this was a food stamp investigation. Everybody, including most of the defendants thought it had something to do with illegal gambling. The TV stations showed up out on the street. It was frickin' cool! LVMPD started running everybody in the place for wants and warrants and they hauled a few guys, unrelated to our investigation out the door in handcuffs—you've got to pay those traffic tickets, you know?

Paul and I had to start preparing for the trials of the defendants; we had hours and hours of tape-recorded conversations of the illegal transactions. These tapes had to be copied for the defense, transcripts had to be made of all the conversations. Back in the eighties at the Las Vegas Resident Agency we didn't have the computers investigators have nowadays. It was a massive undertaking and it kept us busy for weeks.

All thirty-five defendants ended up pleading guilty, but not without some drama. There is always drama. We slowly ticked off the guilty pleas on the individual cases, but six of the defendants from the Leroy's case still hadn't changed their plea to guilty. On trial day the AUSA and I carried boxes and boxes of evidence into the courtroom. We had spent hours and hours preparing for trial. Paul was in Las Vegas for a couple of weeks helping us prepare the presentation of evidence.

The six defendants were sitting at the defense table with six different defense lawyers. As we stacked the boxes of evidence around the prosecutor's table, I could see the defendants squirming in their chairs. Some were in whispered discussions with their attorneys. Paul walked in and sat with us at the prosecution table... more whispers. The US district court judge walked in and took the bench. The first day of the trial was about to begin.

One attorney jumped up and to address the court. His client wanted to change his plea. A second attorney rose to address the court; his client wanted to change his plea. Pretty soon Jimmy jumped out of his seat and screamed, "I'm guilty!" His attorney grabbed him by the arm and pulled him down into his chair. The judge banged the gavel, "Order! Order in the court!"

One by one they all changed their plea. The judge had the defendants line up in front of the bench. Poor Jimmy was hopping from foot to foot; he was bouncing around like a squirrel! I've never seen a defendant so anxious to plead guilty, it was almost as if he thought the judge would only accept change of pleas from the first guy to speak up and the rest are shit out of luck. *Jimmy, relax pal, your turn is coming.* There is something about a federal courtroom that is very intimidating to your average run-of-the mill crook. This ain't traffic court, that's for sure, and Jimmy was more than ready to throw himself upon the mercy of the court.

Finally, it was over. We all breathed a sigh of relief…it had been a monster of a case. Paul went back to Sacramento and I'd never see him again.

* * *

As the case had progressed, I tried to talk Paul into applying with the Secret Service—he would have made a really good Secret Service agent. Paul was tempted, but he decided his family wouldn't be able to handle all the travel a Secret Service agent is faced with. This, from a guy who spent about ninety days on temporary duty in Las Vegas. Go figure!

Those who work in other agencies have always held the misconception that Secret Service agents work excessive duty, though it is true to an extent. But in my career I never left the Redhead for ninety frickin' days! True, Secret Service agents have

Long

to relocate and can't spend their entire career in their hometown, and that was always the sticking point. Generally speaking, Secret Service agents are faced with a move to a big field office and a permanent protection assignment. You're looking at a minimum of two relocations during your career. And then those presidential campaigns—twenty-one days on and twenty-one days off.

Years later, after I'd moved on from Las Vegas, Paul decided to leave the USDA—I guess those ninety-day temps to the hither lands of their geographical jurisdiction were too much for him. Paul transferred to the Department of Housing and Urban Development IG. They sent him to Oklahoma City.

On April 19, 1995, my buddy Paul Broxterman reported for work at the federal building in Oklahoma City and was killed by Timothy McVeigh. The Secret Service lost six employees that day, including Alan Whicher, one of my former supervisors on the presidential protective detail at the White House. I was at the White House working day shift protecting the life of President Clinton and I remember watching the news reports in the Secret Service command post, tucked in the lower level of the West Wing. I lost six colleagues that day, and little did I know I'd also lost a very good friend.

In 1999 the Redhead and I stopped in Oklahoma City while on a cross-country vacation. We walked through the Murrah Federal Building Memorial, a very beautiful scene including empty chairs in a grass field, waterfalls, and monuments. I walked around to pay my respects to the memory of my six lost colleagues, and when I came upon Paul's memorial I unexpectedly broke down and started sobbing like a little kid. I was a little embarrassed. I didn't anticipate that would be my reaction. I had some great memories of working with Paul Broxterman. He was an outstanding criminal investigator and one hell of an undercover agent.

* * *

I got back into the groove of working out at the gym with Donnie and the Beaver at oh-dark-thirty again. The Beaver and I resumed our quest for the best cheeseburger in Las Vegas. I didn't know it, but my days of working criminal cases in Las Vegas were about to come to an end.

Chapter 13

Forty-Two

Finally the day came when I brought the home the good news that we were leaving the Great American Desert. Good-bye Glitter Gulch and the constant sound of coins dropping into tin trays. Adios, dust, sand, wind, and sweltering hot sunshine. The Redhead was ecstatic, to say the least. I was on my way to Washington, DC, and eventually, the Presidential Protective Detail.

I was lucky enough to spend close to seven years on the President's detail, comprising two tours on PPD with Forty-One, Forty-Two, and Forty-Three; that's George H. W. Bush, Bill Clinton, and George W. Bush. My first PPD assignment was as a shift agent and my second was as a first line supervisor.

I settled in to the protection routine of working a shift...two weeks of days, two weeks of afternoons, two weeks of midnights, and a two-week training cycle. I actually found I had much more time at home than I did working criminal cases in Las Vegas. Go figure. On the detail we worked our eight-hour shift and went home, which was awesome! No unpredictable telephone calls in the middle of the night…on the shift we called it "eight and skate."

In August of 1993, President Clinton took his first vacation as President. We went to Arkansas for a few days, then to Vail, Colorado, and finally to Martha's Vineyard. We were at our morning shift meeting, on the last day before leaving the Arkansas lakeside estate of Mr. Tyson (the chicken Tyson) where the President was staying, and the shift leader was briefing us on the President's itinerary for the next few days in Vail, and one of the scheduled activities was that the President and Chelsea would be horseback riding.

PPD has to maintain a good solid inner perimeter around the President at all times and that includes all his activities in public. If the President is a skier, we had to have agents who could ski with him. If the President was a runner, we had to have agents that could run with him and if the President was an expert horseman, like President Reagan, we had to have expert horsemen to ride with him.

When Reagan was President, PPD used to send agents to the US Park Police riding school, and that always seemed like a big deal—to ride with the President. During Reagan's tenure in the White House, quite a few PPD agents attended this riding school. When George H. W. Bush became President, the "riding qualified" agents slowly left the detail and since President Bush didn't ride, there was no need to train additional agents.

"Can anybody here ride a horse?" the shift leader now asked us. I'm still the new guy on the shift, I'm an operational kind of guy…I'm not going to sit in the follow-up when I could be protecting the man, am I? So, of course I raise my hand. *Hell, yeah! I can ride a horse.* I look around and my hand is the only one in the air. *Oops.* Okay, so I have ridden horses before…the trail-ride type of horseback riding, that kind of horseback riding. I am not an expert horseman, by any means…I don't even know how to saddle a frickin' horse, for Pete's sake. But guess what? The shift leader didn't inquire as to my level of horsemanship: nope, he just asked if anyone could ride. "Okay," he said. "You're riding with the President." And a cowboy was born.

That ride in Vail was a simple trail ride along a mountain path. The kind of tourist activity you'd take your kids on while you were on vacation in Vail, Colorado. And back at our shift meeting when I unhesitatingly raised my hand, that's what I kind of figured this "horseback riding" with Chelsea and President Clinton was all about. Nevertheless, I was a bit relieved to see this was a "trail" ride with wranglers leading the way, the horses walking as we sat atop saddles. However, being the Type A person I am (like all agents), I really got into the ride and decided to act like I knew how to ride a horse.

When I was a teenager, I remember my dad giving me some really great advice, "Son, if you ever find yourself in a situation where you're not supposed to be," he told me, "Just act like you know what you are doing and no one will question you." So, I took what little knowledge of riding a horse I had, visualized how a "real" horseman would command and direct his horse, and did it.

After a few days in Vail we hit Martha's Vineyard for the rest of the President's vacation. And wouldn't you know it…Chelsea and the President decide to go horseback riding again. And of course I was assigned to ride with them on another easy "trail" ride. All of a sudden I'm the designated horseback rider for the President!

Later that fall, the President was in Billings, Montana, for an event and a little R&R. You guessed it…he's going to a large ranch to ride horses. So, of course, I'm assigned to ride with him. After all, I *am* the designated rider. I was working the shift and when we arrived at the ranch the trail hand asked me if I rode western or English. *Western? English? Holy shit.* "Uh, western,"

I said. He handed me a saddle. *What now? I've got to saddle this horse? I have no clue.* My shift leader, bless his soul, came to my rescue, as I stood with my mouth agape and a saddle in my arms. The rancher was giving the President a walking tour of the barn, stables, and house.

"Can you saddle the horse, please? I need all my men to stay with the President," said the shift leader. Whew! Saved again.

The PPD SAIC, myself, and one other agent (a new member of the shift, whom I'm sure really knew how to ride) were riding with President Clinton. It was the wide-open range, not a trail ride, and I was a bit nervous. Will my ruse be exposed? Will I be embarrassed in front of the President? The boss came to my aid once again. The riding party was in a wide valley between two ridgelines. He sent me to the south ridge and the other agent to the north ridge. "Give us plenty of room, boys," he told us. "Ride the flanks up on the ridge tops." Which was close to a half a mile away. Perfect, just me and old "Bull's-eye" protecting the south flank. I took off to the south and rode up to the ridge—from there I could just barely see the outline of the riding party way down in the valley. To the south I could see for fifty miles. It was beautiful. I rode parallel to President Clinton along the ridgeline out of sight of the party.

Everything was going great, Bull's-eye and I, clopping along the open prairie. Then we turned for home to retrace our steps. The closer we got to the barn, the faster old Bull's-eye walked, then trotted, then ran, then a full out gallop.

"Whoa, Bull's-eye!" I screamed, "Whoa!" The horse did not respond to my commands and in fact, it seemed like he increased his speed. I didn't have a clue how to slow down this horse, other than to pull back on the reigns and holler my lungs out. My legs were flapping out of the stirrups and we were going so fast over the bumpy ground, I had no hope of getting them back in place. I held on for dear life. I ended up grabbing the saddle horn with both hands and praying. And I didn't fall. As we descended the ridgeline toward the highway and the barn on the other side of the highway, Bull's-eye actually started slowing down and I got my feet in the stirrups and a good grip on the reins. We slowed to a walk; just about the time President Clinton, the SAIC, and the rest of the riding party rounded the bend at the bottom of the ridgeline to cross over the highway to the stables. I had pulled it off again. That was my last ride with President Clinton, which was probably a good thing.

* * *

Working golf courses with President Clinton was always interesting. I met some of the nicest people in the world on a golf course, especially the homeowners who lived along the course. But there is always an exception...

One morning, somewhere on an out-of-town trip, we were on a golf course. We could have been in Arkansas, on Martha's Vineyard, or in Timbuktu, for all I remember. I was working the right front flank out in front of the President. Two homeowners were standing next to the fairway and I walked up to size them up. Talking to people is the easiest way to determine their state of mind and attitude toward the President. I was thinking chances are these two are not a threat to the President. Nice house. Dressed sharp. Enjoying their morning coffee watching President Clinton golf down the fairway behind their house. So I walk up to these folks and said, "Good morning. How are you today?"

Now, most people get a thrill talking to a Secret Service agent, some folks are more interested in asking questions to an agent than they are in seeing the President. The man doesn't say shit. The lady, with an edge in her voice says, "This is our property." *Okay; I figured it was.* Then she snarls, "You can't tell me to move," and she points at her toes. "This is my property line right here." She's got her frickin' toes on the imaginary property line.

"Okay, I said, "Nice house."

"You can't tell me to move," she says.

"Why should I ask you to move?" I ask.

Now she gets really snarky, "You can't! My son is an attorney."

"Oh, that's great," I said. By this time President Clinton has moved up the fairway and it's time for me to move forward. "Well that's awesome," I say to the lady. "We need good prosecutors out there to put assholes in jail. You have a nice day."

I figured her for a liberal right away. One thing I've noticed over the years with the difference between liberals and conservatives. When a liberal sees a cop they immediately get defensive. "Fuck the police!" When a conservative sees a cop they think, "Thank God, the police are here!" Just an observation.

President Clinton was a pretty good golfer and he definitely loved the game. It seemed like he played every weekend, sometimes more than once a weekend. I even remember him hitting the links on some weekday afternoons. I guess when the golf bug bites, you have to scratch. On one golf outing President Clinton was playing with former President Ford and a world-famous tour golfer.

When President Clinton would finish a round of golf, the staff would bring the White House Press Pool out to the eighteenth green to watch him finish up…throwing them a bone, so to speak, since the staff wouldn't allow the press on the course while he was playing. After he finished the round, President Clinton always made a big show of adding up his score. He'd sit in the golf cart and cypher that scorecard like it was the monthly unemployment numbers. Some guy from the press pool would always shout out to President Clinton, "What'd you shoot today, Mr. President?"

I had no idea what he shot that day, or any other day for that matter. I wasn't there to keep score; I was there to let him live to hit them another day. I was standing right next to former President Ford when a pool reporter shouted out to President Clinton. "What'd you shoot today?"

"Eighty-three," said President Clinton. "I shot an eighty-three today."

The press pool reporters continued shouting questions to the President, and former President Ford leans over and whispers to me. "Add ten to that."

* * *

Over the years, I get asked a lot of questions about the job. I've found it very interesting that when I meet someone for the first time, perhaps at a neighborhood party or any social event, everybody— and I mean everybody—Democrats, Republicans, wacked-out lefties, wound-too-tight right-wingers, and all those folks in between, including foreigners—all ask me the same question. And I know exactly what you are thinking right now, and maybe the only reason you are reading this book…what is Hillary *really* like?

It is amazing to me that even the staunchest Democrat wants to know, even folks you can tell just by looking at them that they love Hillary will want to know, what is she really like? I can understand a Republican asking me that question. But her ardent supporters? *Really?* My answer? "Well I was never assigned to the First Lady's detail, so I wasn't around her that much." And then, I change the subject.

The second question is always, "Who was your favorite President?" Obviously, they want to hear me say their favorite among those I worked with, just to confirm their individual political beliefs. So I always answer with, "Abraham Lincoln."

I will say this—the members of the Bush family, every one of them, were some of the nicest people I've ever met. And President

Clinton was always nice to me; he is a very charming man and a very intelligent man. I was always amazed at how he could remember people, or at least make them believe he remembered them. We'd be working a rope line with President Clinton and inevitably someone would say to him something like, "I met you in Podunk, Arkansas, in 1989," and in those few seconds of interaction, that person would be convinced he remembered them. Maybe he did. But I do know one thing—he remembered me.

Years after President Clinton left office, I was the ASAIC of the Seattle Field Office. Seattle had a huge geographical jurisdiction—Alaska, western Canada, northern Idaho, Montana, Oregon, and Washington State. Anytime a Secret Service–protected person visited that geographic area, agents from Seattle were involved with the protection of those people. When Mrs. Clinton was a senator, she and Senators John McCain, Lindsey Graham, and Susan Collins made a trip to inspect the Prudhoe Bay oil fields in Alaska. This was during a drilling controversy, and Congress was debating opening up more acreage for drilling.

I went to Barrow, Alaska with the Seattle FO advance team to make preliminary security arrangements. It was in early July and it snowed the day we arrived. A few days later, the senators arrived via private jet at Barrow International Airport. From there, they choppered over the oil fields and then came back to Barrow; I got on the plane with them and flew back to Anchorage. When we arrived in Anchorage, we motorcaded the senators to the Kenai Peninsula for some meetings. A few days later, we made it back to Anchorage for wheels up. On this particular day, Senator Clinton was meeting former president Clinton at the Anchorage airport. They were flying via private jet to Hawaii for a vacation.

As we motorcaded into the private jet side of the airport, former President Clinton was waiting planeside for Mrs. Clinton. He was standing on the ramp right next to the boarding ladder, just him and one of his Secret Service agents. Senator Clinton's detail leader directed the motorcade agent to go directly to the office of the fixed base operator (FBO) for a stop before boarding. Senator Clinton had to make an important telephone call. All the agents went in with Senator Clinton. I was riding in the police tail car and I got out of the car and stood next to it.

Suddenly, I hear my name being called from a distance. *What?* I'm looking around to see who is calling my name. I glanced over toward the private jet and former president Clinton is waving and calling out to me. *Are you kidding me?* He started walking in my direction and I met him halfway. He wanted to know how I was doing. "Are you still in Seattle?" he asked me. Unbelievable.

We had a nice short conversation before Senator Clinton walked out of the FBO and onto the plane. I could not believe President Clinton remembered me, much less my name. It had been at least seven or eight years since I'd been assigned to his detail and I was just one of many, many shift agents assigned to PPD during his tenure as President. As a shift agent I had very little verbal interaction with a president, supervisors verbally interact with a president all the time, but we "humps" just did our job and kept quiet. So I didn't converse much with President Clinton; but I did make him scream once…

I was on the working shift on a trip to Florida. We were working the day shift and at three in the morning my hotel room telephone rang. It was my Shift Leader. That's never a good call. President Clinton had hurt his knee the night before and he was in the hospital. The day shift needed to get to the hospital ASAP to push the midnight shift, as we were leaving for Andrews AFB shortly.

The President needed surgery on his knee and we were going to motorcade directly from Andrews to Bethesda Naval Hospital.

President Clinton was lying in a hospital bed; the First Lady, some senior staff, and a doctor were by his side. His leg was immobilized in a hip-to-ankle brace. Now we had to figure out how to get him into the Beast (the presidential limo) and out to Air Force One. So we did what all good Secret Service agents do—we practiced the movement. We put one of the shift agents in a wheel chair next to the right rear door of the Beast and tried to get him in the backseat. It became clear there was no way we could get him or the President into the Beast, so with time running out the shift leader said, "Let's try the follow-up" (the Secret Service suburban that the shift agents ride during a motorcade).

The SAIC and a local doc wheeled the President out of the hospital and to the departure point. We put a huge pile of pillows on the rear seat of the follow-up, because the President was going to have to lean against the left rear door with his immobilized leg resting on the bench seat. The shift leader had me get in the follow-up as they backed the wheelchair up to the right rear door. I sat on the right rear seat, facing out and grasp President Clinton under his arms, with my arms under his armpits and my hands clasped together on his chest to lift him off the wheelchair and slide him into position in the backseat. As I lifted up, President Clinton let out a scream in pain and grabbed his knee. I guess I pulled a little too hard; but, I sure as shit didn't want to drop the President on the sidewalk! I eased him down on the wheelchair and we started over, this time with two agents on each side of him and me from the back. The second time worked like a charm, as we eased him into position with the pillows.

President Clinton rode to Air Force One in the backseat of the follow-up and the shift agents rode in the Beast. That was probably the only time in the history of the Secret Service that the President rode in the follow-up and the shift rode in the limo.

The Beast...now that was a car! We called it the Beast because it was so frickin' big and heavy compared to previous presidential limos. The ultimate protection limo. It was awesome.

* * *

When I was on PPD, shift agents would spend their first year or
so working the shift protecting the President. After that first year
we would be rotated to one of four other specialty assignments on
PPD. We'd spend a year or so on that specialty assignment and then
rotate back to the working shift for the remainder of our tour of
duty. When my time came, I was notified I was going to the First
Lady's detail. Sure as shootin' when the next weeks shift schedule
came out, I was gone from my shift to the First Lady's detail.
And starting the week out right I was scheduled to start my new
assignment Sunday on day shift. I was on paper. It was carved in
stone. It was set in concrete...

"Don't believe until its on paper." That's what us T-men always
said. With the government things change, so if it ain't on paper, it
doesn't mean shit.

I was on a day off, a good old Dee-Oh the Saturday before that
change to the First Lady's detail. The Redhead and I were sitting
around, sippin' a beer and firin' up the old BBQ. The telephone
rings. It's my shift leader—until midnight, away—and then I'd have
a new shift leader from the First Lady's detail. When your shift
leader calls you at home it can't be good news.

It was a good news, bad news deal. He told me Sunday would
also be my day off and Monday report to the Transportation Section
(TS). It seems there was a last-minute change. My shift leader told
me the staff got involved with this switch and when one of the First
Lady's staffers found out my shift mate, Danny, was going to TS
next week they called the SAIC. "We really were hoping Danny
would be assigned to Mrs. Clinton," they said.

Done! Danny goes to the First Lady's detail and I go to TS...a
simple switch of personnel. I mean a body is a body right? It turned

out to be one of the absolutely best deals for me during my entire career.

TS agents conduct presidential motorcade advances and drive the President's limo and various other Secret Service vehicles in a PPD motorcade. It is hard work...it is high visibility...a motorcade advance is complicated, one of the hardest assignments an agent gets, second only to lead advances (good luck getting one of my pals from the First Lady's detail to admit that, but it is a true as the Vegas sky is blue).

The first thing I had to do was complete the Protective Operations Driving Course (PODC) training. And this was the absolute best training I ever received. PODC teaches the agent how to drive. Really drive. Drive hard, drive fast, and drive safe. We had IROC-Zs for our training cars, and I had some experience with an IROC-Z—geez! If I'd been through PODC back in my Vegas days... well, it's probably better that I hadn't at that point in my career.

What are you going to do if your driving forward and the lane is blocked? Perhaps an explosion at an intersection? An RPG to the vehicle in the front? No problem, just throw the vehicle in reverse, do a 180-degree turn and drive as hard and as fast in the opposite direction as you safely can...and do this maneuver in one lane of traffic. The good old J-turn. Absolutely some of the most fun you can have in a car! And it's surprisingly easy to do. You just have to know how.

Years later, when my daughter was getting her driver's license, she made a bet that if she made a perfect score on the test, I'd teach her to do a "J" turn...she came very, very close.

Driving the presidential limo was a great honor and a huge responsibility—one of my TS buddies used to introduce his fellow TS agents to civilians with by saying, "I want you to meet Agent So-and-So, he is one of twelve people in the world authorized to drive the President of the United States." That's an exclusive club.

I remind my family of this regularly when we are on vacation road trips. If the Redhead makes a comment about my driving, I just remind her, "Relax, I used to drive the President of the United States."

Every time the President moves anywhere, even frickin' walking; there is a TS agent conducting a motorcade advance. The TS agent works with the local police to plan routes, secure the routes, and have plan A, B, C, and even D in his/her hip pocket. I was doing a TS advance in Albuquerque once and after days of planning the White House advance staff decided to use Marine One for a movement to a venue that was a long motorcade from his last stop. My police counterpart was so relieved there would be a helicopter movement instead of a long distance motorcade. "Not so fast partner," I said, "This will not make the motorcade advance easier, it will make it harder and more complicated."

"How so?" he asked.

"Well, now we need two motorcade packages—one to get him to the takeoff LZ (landing zone) and one to pick him up at the landing LZ." When you are transporting the President, nothing, absolutely nothing, is easy.

By the luck of the draw, I was the TS advance agent for the motorcade of President Clinton with the Kennedy family for the funeral of Jackie Kennedy Onassis. Her burial was at Arlington National Cemetery outside Washington, DC, next to her late husband, President John F. Kennedy. We motorcaded from the south grounds of the White House to Reagan National Airport in Northern Virginia, where President Clinton met the Kennedy family and casket. We took her up George Washington Parkway to Arlington. George Washington Parkway was lined with mourners and media. It was a very somber moment in my Secret Service career.

* * *

Doing a foreign motorcade advance was always a big challenge. Obviously the language barrier is an issue, but dealing with foreign countries and their diplomatic protocol would give anyone a headache. I did a TS advance in Paris for President Clinton and the diplomatic protocol was a nightmare. We were at the French president's residence for a state dinner. It went late into the night. All of a sudden, the Secret Service lead advance agent tells me the French president just invited President and Mrs. Clinton to the Louvre for a midnight private tour. One problem. Diplomatic protocol called for the French president to say good-bye to the visiting president when he leaves the residence and protocol called for the French president to be at the Louvre so he can be the first to greet the arriving visitor.

"Can they motorcade together?" I asked.

"No, absolutely not." I was told by the White House Staff Lead Advance. Now this is a problem.

"Can we motorcade to the US ambassador's residence, stand by, and wait for the French president to arrive at the Louvre?"

"No. Absolutely not," the staff lead tells me.

Great, now what am I supposed to do? Drive in circles? And then I got a great idea. "Why don't we motorcade over to Notre Dame Cathedral, stop by the Seine River for a view of the lights of Paris?" It was close to two o'clock in the morning and the Paris cops told me the streets at Notre Dame were deserted. The Secret Service lead and the SAIC said, "Good idea; let's do that to kill some time."

So off we went to Notre Dame. There is a pedestrian bridge over the Seine River right near Notre Dame. We stopped the motorcade there. The President and Mrs. Clinton got out of the limo and walked out onto the pedestrian bridge. They spent about twenty minutes enjoying the view and then we loaded them up and drove to the Louvre. The French president was waiting to greet President and Mrs. Clinton for the arrival and the private tour of the Louvre.

The next morning the front pages of all the Paris newspapers had a huge photo of President and Mrs. Clinton strolling hand in hand on the bridge—how romantic! Banner headlines! Paris! The city of lights and romance! And it was all my idea. *Your welcome, White House staff.*

* * *

After my tour in TS I went back to the shift and started doing lead advances for PPD visits. I loved doing leads, because they were always very challenging and required us to "think out of the box." I did a lot of lead advances and for some reason, just the luck of the draw, I guess, it seemed my staff lead advance counterpart was usually the same guy. He was a Hollywood movie producer who volunteered his time to travel and complete the staff lead advances. As a matter of fact he was the staff lead advance for my TS advance in Paris, he was the one who was so difficult about President and Mrs. Clinton leaving the French state dinner for the Louvre tour. This guy was a pain in the ass and (usually) very uncooperative about our security needs.

He and I were paired up as the respective lead advances for a President Clinton visit to St. Petersburg, Russia. He was always coming up with harebrained ideas that were extremely challenging from a security perspective. The President was going to tour a local St. Petersburg museum, exit a side door on the street, walk three blocks along the sidewalk, enter a small park, and visit St. Basil's Cathedral for a private tour. Then the staff wanted to motorcade him across a wide boulevard to an open-air flea market for an "off the record" (OTR) stop to mingle with the local folks. Both of these movements were potentially dangerous and extremely challenging.

When the site advance agent and I started looking at the walk along the sidewalk we were both very concerned about the high ground issues—it was a wide street with two and three story row houses along the far side of the street. I argued for a motorcade to the cathedral. But, Mr. Hollywood Producer said, "No, we can't do that! Absolutely not! It'll ruin the photo shots by the press! We want him walking to the park and the cathedral."

I knew this was extremely dangerous. It would be impossible to cover this walk along the sidewalk to the park from the threat of a sniper. Once in the treed park we would be okay—there were lots of trees for blocking the line of sight.

I told the site advance agent to get some buses, big busses to park on the street blocking the line of sight from the two and three story buildings across the street. I knew Mr. Hollywood Producer would not go for this tunnel along the sidewalk; it would ruin his photo shot. I waited for the right moment, when Mr. Hollywood Producer was preoccupied with other issues and approached him. I told him the walk was very dangerous and I'd have to be creative to cover those three blocks. "No problem," he said and he got back into his discussion with the other staff.

When President Clinton exited the side door of the museum, he was met by a wall of buses parked along the curb. Hollywood Producer went berserk. President Clinton was engaged in a deep conversation with whoever was accompanying him on the walk and I don't think he even noticed the buses. But Mr. Hollywood Producer was pissed off! I didn't really care, because I had successfully mitigated the long-range sniper threat.

After the tour of the Cathedral, we loaded up in the Beast for the OTR at the flea market.

I was very worried about this flea market stop. It was an OTR, and theoretically, for an OTR, no one knows the President is going to make the stop, thus the odds of an assassin lying in wait are slim. But still, a flea market in a shady part of town is not ideal. After Mr. Hollywood Producer told me about the proposed OTR, I took one of the advance team agents with me and we strolled through the flea market to size it up. We didn't like the looks of things. It appeared to be a haven for crooks, thugs, and other non desirable characters of St. Petersburg.

This OTR was going to be a challenge and the working shift would have to be on alert for problems. Fortunately, the President was behind schedule and as we loaded into the motorcade at St. Basil's Cathedral, Mr. Hollywood Producer told me to skip the OTR and motorcade directly to the next scheduled event.

* * *

During the 1996 reelection campaign of President Clinton, his staff decided he should do a whistle-stop train trip to the convention in Chicago and I was assigned as the lead advance. I started working on that advance the Monday after the Fourth of July 1995. It consumed most of my time until we arrived at the shores of Lake Michigan for the Democratic National Convention in late August.

One of the first things we did was ride the rails for the proposed route of travel. As luck would have it, once again, the Mr. Hollywood Producer was my staff lead advance counterpart. We boarded a private "charter" train in Huntington, West Virginia; this train had three cars—the engine, a support rail car, and a luxury private coach. It was a small group—me, Mr. Hollywood Producer, another senior White House staffer, one of the PPD ASAICs, a representative from Amtrak, and a representative from the train company that operated the rail line.

We would make stops at small towns; get out of our private train and look around with the staff for them to decide if this small town would be included in a reelection rally for the presidential train whistle stop. If the staff liked the look of the small town, we would make decisions about where to stop the train, where to set a stage and build a crowd…then jump back on the charter and whizz off to the next potential stop. All of this took about twenty minutes. I didn't have much time to inspect the potential venues and give final approval to the staff. But at this point in my PPD career I had completed many site advances and I could visualize the security setup, make a quick sketch of the venue, and calculate a "ballpark" estimate of how many cops and how many agents it would take to secure the venue before we moved on to the next small town they where they wanted to hold an event.

At one stop, we had the "charter" pull off on a side rail and we walked over to a Dairy Queen for lunch. We were sitting in the restaurant that was right next to the tracks with a street crossing the tracks. I was sitting with the two train guys and they were telling me how dangerous grade crossings were. They were telling me about how many cars get hit by trains every year, usually because the drivers of those cars try and beat the track warning barriers as they start to come down to stop traffic.

Sure as shit, as we are sitting there, we hear the *ding-ding-ding* of the track barriers, with the flashing red lights and watch the wooden arm as it starts to activate to block the street so a train can pass. We were looking out the window and I'll be darned if a flat bed stake truck tried to sneak under the barrier arms as they are coming down. The first arm comes down and gets wedged between the cab and the bed of the truck.

Now the truck is stuck with the hood and front wheels on the track and the loud whistle of the approaching train blaring in the distance. We dropped our burgers and ran out to the grade crossing. I'm standing there thinking, *this is going to be ugly when that speeding train hits that truck*. The two train guys got under the wooden barrier arm; lifted it up and the truck driver sped forward across the tracks. Whoosh. The train goes by and disaster is adverted. It was a close call for that driver. His lucky day…having two train experts sitting fifty feet from the crossing. Those two guys knew what to do and they reacted quickly enough to save the truck driver from total disaster and sure death. I was totally impressed, but these fellas just shrugged it off as another day on the tracks.

After the route was set and the stops were identified, I made numerous return trips to each city along the route with other members of the advance team to finalize our security plan. We had over eighteen hundred grade crossings along the route that traversed five states, West Virginia, Kentucky, Ohio, Michigan, and Indiana. I made a note to check and double check the police posts at each grade crossing—not only for the assassins waiting to sabotage the train, but some dumb ass trying to get across the tracks to the grocery store for a gallon of milk.

The train ended up being one quarter of a mile long. The staff must have had every donor in each of the states we were traversing on that train at one stop or another. It was almost comical. When we stopped the train at one of the predetermined small towns for a rally, the staff would unload a bunch of donors that rode from the last stop and reload the cars with donors from the current stop. I guess folks just get a kick out of telling their social circle all about the time *they* rode the 1996 presidential reelection campaign train. What's really funny is that during the three-day trip, President Clinton only made one sojourn from the presidential car up through rest of the train to meet and greet these folks. So the vast majority never saw him up close. I guess I shouldn't be so cynical, but when you stand next to the President of the United States every day, it doesn't seem like a big deal. But that's the life of a Secret Service agent.

I felt bad for the guy who donated the use of his private rail car. It was a beautiful, old 1920s restored car. The outside rear had the porch and railing like you see in all the old photos from when this was the only way to travel across country. This thing was a gem and the guy that owned it was a super nice guy. We were about a day from the President's arrival in Huntington for the departure and good old Mr. Owner was under the impression he would be riding the rails inside his "loaned" private car with the President.

My staff lead counterpart, Mr. Hollywood Producer, got wind that the owner was planning to ride in the back and he put the kibosh on that real quick. I remember a heated discussion between the two, right beside the private car. He relented and agreed to ride up front with the straphangers, but he wasn't happy.

Later that same day one of the staff press aides was inspecting the rear patio in order to find the optimum photo angle to place the press during stops where President Clinton would address the throngs of supporters if he made a speech from the rear of the private car. You know, like the famous photo of President Harry Truman on the porch of his private train.

Well, the top overhang of the private car had a scalloped awning around it. The White House staff press aide didn't like that scalloped awning. Blocking too much of the "shot." So he called a welder from the train depot and told him to cut it off with the old blowtorch—cut right through the metal and remove the scalloping. Only problem was he didn't bother to run this major modification by the owner.

I'd become pretty good buddies with the owner and to be honest, I thought the staff was treating him like the hired help, so I kind of put the bug in his ear about the welder and his blowtorch. He went completely bullshit. Absolutely crazy. He threatened to pull his private car out of the show entirely if they so much as touched the thing. I'm sure a lot of this reaction to this news was the result of his disappointment with being told he would not be riding in his private car with the President; but what ever the reason, he was *pissed*.

Finally, Mr. Hollywood Producer compromised with him—the staff removes the awning scalloping, agrees to have it replaced when the show is over, and Mr. Owner gets to ride in his car with the President. Like most folks, he didn't envision the entourage that accompanies the President wherever he goes. Once we started the train, the owner quickly realized there was no room in the private car—what with the senior staff, military aide, Secret Service agents, speechwriters. Shit, it was packed. I spent most of the trip standing on the rear platform of the private car, just to be out of the way. A few hours after launch, the owner went up to the "public" cars and found a nice seat for the rest of the three days.

The three-day train trip through five states was a complete success. Every one of those eighteen hundred grade crossings had a cop or at least the local rural volunteer fire department posted when the train went by.

* * *

By the time President Clinton was starting his second term of office, I was a senior agent on the shift and I'd advanced to be named the number one whip on my shift (the whip fills in for the shift leader on his days off). On January 20, 1996, all the whips from all the shifts were given the honor of walking along the Beast for the motorcade parade from the Capitol swearing-in ceremony down Pennsylvania Avenue to the White House. It was quite an honor. I was the top of the food chain on PPD.

But somehow, the job has a way to humble us all. After the parade was over, I was given a post standing assignment later that evening at one of the *numerous* presidential inaugural balls. The Secret Service site advance agent posted me in the boiler room in the basement of the venue. Me, a steel folding chair, and this huge, loud steam boiler. For six hours. I went from the pinnacle to the basement all in one day.

Chapter 14

The Frenchman and The Dude

Freddie, Bernie, and Irving have a very nice fingerprint lab and database. For decades criminals and non-criminals have had their fingerprints sent to the FBI lab for classification and inclusion in their database. Anyone in the United States who has had their fingerprints taken by a law enforcement agency for any reason—arrest, job application, background investigation, whatever, those fingerprints end up at the FBI lab, where they are classified and checked to see if they are of record with a unique FBI assigned number. If not, Freddie, Bernie, and Irving will assign a new, unique FBI number to that set of prints, which of course, is tied to one individual and one individual only.

Theoretically.

About three or four months after President Clinton's second inauguration, the Redhead and I sold the house, packed, up and moved west. The Seattle Field Office had an opening for a GS-13 agent and we felt it was time to leave the East Coast. Seattle seemed like a good destination for us—L.A. was too big, San Francisco was too expensive, and Vegas...as much as the Redhead hated Glitter Gulch, that wasn't an option.

One rainy afternoon, I was sitting at my desk in the Seattle Field Office working on a case and I received an interesting telephone call from a Tacoma, Washington, coin dealer. He was one of those guys who advertised in the back pages of a magazine selling gold and silver commemorative coin sets. "Guaranteed one troy ounce of real gold minted in a beautiful rendition of the timber wolf, polar bear or American eagle!" You know the ones.

He told me he had recently sold six sets of gold coins to six different people all at the same address. He said he usually only sells six of these unique sets in a one-year period. He gave me the address and the six different credit card numbers. I contacted the issuing banks and found that all six were unauthorized transactions with ninety-six hundred dollars in fraud. Worth looking into...

The address was a commercial mail drop in Bellevue, Washington, and was opened by Henri Stefano as a business mailbox. The owner told me Stefano presented an international passport as identification. *An international passport? Are you kidding me?*

The owner said Stefano had received quite a few letters and packages addressed to three or four different names. He could provide no further information. I contacted a detective at the Bellevue Police Department who worked white-collar crime. The detective checked his files and told me Stefano was not of record with his department. He agreed to assist me with the investigation.

A few days later I received a telephone call from the coin dealer, he told me they had received another order for the same gold coin set and to be shipped to the same address. The dealer told me one of his employees had shipped the package for delivery on Saturday.

I contacted the detective at Bellevue PD and advised him of the situation. This had the potential to be a long, drawn-out surveillance of the twenty-four-hour access mail drop business. There was no guarantee the suspect would show up during normal business hours on Saturday to claim the package. I had a family commitment with the Redhead on Saturday and I didn't want to disappoint her again. I'd done that enough in my career already. I told the detective that I would be available about four or five Saturday afternoon and I'd get out there as soon as possible.

The Bellevue PD set up the surveillance of the commercial mail drop business and the suspect showed up and claimed the package right before closing time. Officers from the Bellevue PD made the arrest and transported him to the Bellevue PD. Perfect timing! My pager went off as I pulled into our driveway. I kissed the Redhead good-bye and told her I'd see her when I see her...she'd heard that line before.

After his arrest Stefano refused to tell the arresting officers if he was driving a car or how he'd arrived at the commercial mail drop. The detectives found a set of car keys in his pocket and an electronic key for a hotel room. They were able to locate the car in the strip mall parking lot by using the key fob. The detective had the car towed to the PD impound lot and secured as evidence.

The suspect claimed his name was Henri Stefano and he was from France. He refused to tell us where he lived or where he was staying or any further information. We advised him of his Miranda rights and he declined to answer questions without an attorney present. I contacted the duty AUSA in Seattle and briefed her on the investigation. She authorized me to arrest Stefano and charge him with credit card fraud.

I wrote an affidavit for an arrest warrant and swore out a John Doe aka Henri Stefano criminal complaint against Stefano. Fortunately, the US magistrate detained him with no bail. Now all I had to do is figure out his real identity. I canvassed just about every hotel in and around Bellevue, Washington, hoping to find where he was staying, but I struck out at every hotel.

During the administrative inventory of the seized Pontiac we found a bill of sale for the car. Stefano paid cash for the new car from a Phoenix, Arizona, car dealership.

I had to leave town soon after that for a protection assignment with the prime minister of Canada. Prime Minister Jean Chretien was spending the Christmas holidays in the United States. He went skiing in Vail, Colorado, and then headed to Phoenix, Arizona, for a week of golf. I was with the prime minister on the links at the Boulders golf course in Scottsdale, Arizona, when my pager went off. Fortunately, we were now in the cell phone age and I just happened to have one.

An agent in Seattle told me the Bellevue PD just called the office to report an extended stay hotel in Bellevue had called the police department to report nonpayment for a room. The manager of the hotel entered the room and saw clothes and personal belongings, but the maid reported she had not seen the guest in over three weeks. The hotel told the Bellevue PD the guest was registered under the name of Henri Stefano.

We only had about two days left until the prime minister returned to Canada, so I told the agent in Seattle to secure and lock the door to the hotel room and as soon as I got back to Seattle I would get a search warrant. Unfortunately, that didn't happen. The agent contacted the duty AUSA and was told all he needed was a grand jury subpoena for the hotel manager to turn over the defendant's property.

And that's what they did…they got a grand jury subpoena and served it on the hotel manager. The agents then cleaned up the room and took all the personal items including clothes, shoes and toiletries, boxed them up and put them in my office. I'd be stuck with that shit for long time.

Back in the early eighties in L.A. when the Secret Service jurisdiction over credit card fraud was in its infancy, we learned that you don't need to seize the refrigerator that was bought with a stolen credit card to make the case. You don't need the ill-gotten goods, you need the actual plastic or the account number and the paper trail of the transaction, and witnesses that saw the suspect use the card or account number. Good old investigative techniques. No AUSA in his or her right mind will wheel a Frigidaire into the courtroom to introduce as evidence. They're going to introduce the paper trail of the purchase.

A defendant's personal property can be a real pain in the ass. It has to be inventoried on a personal property form and signed by the inventorying agent, the defendant and a witness. That's his shit and you have to give it back to him. I learned early on in my investigative career to just seize the evidence and leave his dirty socks on the bedroom floor. But now I was stuck with boxes upon boxes of frickin' clothes—socks, skivvies and dirty blue jeans, smelly tennis shoes and toothpaste. I was standing in my office, the first day after returning from a ten-day protection assignment—I've got a travel voucher to turn in, weekly activity reports that are late, and God only knows what else to get done, but I now had a higher priority task. I had to inventory this shit and get the evidence separated from the personal property, fill out and secure the evidence in the evidence vault, inventory his personal property on the correct form, and secure it in the evidence vault.

The seizing of evidence has to be legal, if is not seized legally a sharp defense attorney—shit, even an attorney fresh out of law school, will file motions to suppress the evidence. This evidence had been seized with a grand jury subpoena and I was very worried we would lose it at a suppression hearing.

Tucked away in those boxes and intermingled with the all clothes was the evidence we needed to prove he'd bought the seven sets of gold coins. But no gold coins. I found MasterCards and Visas, tons of opened and unopened mail—monthly credit card statements from banks. Mr. Stefano was stealing mail right out of your mailbox. Specifically, he was stealing your payment coupon and your check. This guy was trolling through the Seattle suburbs at probably two in the morning, cruising the neighborhood mailboxes looking for the red flag in the up position—your outgoing mail. He was stealing your monthly payment.

The scam was simple. Once he had your payment coupon, he had your address and your account number; your balance and your credit limit. He would open the payment envelope, pull out the payment coupon and fill in the change of address on the coupon, reseal the envelope and mail your payment to the bank. He'd change the address to one of his mail drops, wait a few days for the change of address to be processed by the bank, then call the bank, report the card lost and the bank would be more than happy to FedEx him a replacement card to his new address. *Bingo! He's in business.*

He'd bought that brand-new Pontiac Grand Am in Phoenix with cash. He was making a pretty good living off of your good credit.

I found mail from Santa Fe, Albuquerque, Phoenix, Scottsdale, Las Vegas (they *always* go to Vegas), Sacramento, Portland and the Seattle suburbs. South on Interstate 25 to Interstate 10, a side trip to Las Vegas, Interstate 15 probably to Interstate 5 and north to the Pacific Northwest.

Before I was done contacting banks, I would document tens of thousands of dollars in credit card fraud and a laundry list of innocent victims with their credit rating ruined. *But who was this guy? Henri Stefano from France? No way.*

The FBI's fingerprint lab could positively identify this guy; he had to have a record. So I shipped his fingerprints off to Freddie, Bernie and Irving with an urgent request to expedite this fingerprint examination.

* * *

All Secret Service agents have to find that delicate balance between working criminal cases and protection assignments. Vice President Gore was scheduled to visit Glacier National Park in Montana and I was assigned to help the Vice President's detail with the security advance. Identifying Stefano would have to wait a week or so.

That was going to be a busy week for us in the Seattle Field Office district. President Clinton was scheduled to make a stop in the city of Seattle, then Portland, Oregon and finally a stop in Springfield, Oregon, before flying on the Los Angeles, California. Virtually, every agent in Seattle, Spokane and Portland were involved in some way, shape, or form.

The Vice President's stop in Glacier was a quick one; he was scheduled to make a speech on global warming and was only going to be on the ground for six or seven hours before he was wheels up from the Kalispell, Montana, airport in Air Force Two. He arrived at the Many Glacier Hotel by motorcade from the airport, had a short meeting with some environmental folks and then the group hiked from the Many Glacier Hotel about three miles up the steep valley to the base of the Many Glacier.

The press corps covering the Vice President and some local journalists hiked up the side of the mountain with us. As we walked up the trail, I noticed wooden National Park signs spaced out every so often: 1832, 1865, 1888, 1896, 1900, 1923, etc.; obviously these wooden signs were marking the leading edge of the retreating glacier. When we got to the speech site at the base of the glacier, the press set up their cameras and Mr. Gore commenced his speech.

I was standing behind the press pool on a small ledge with a Glacier National Park Ranger. He was a young fellow and looked like he was just out of college. I was listening to the Vice President's speech and he's droning on and on about the threat of global warming and how the glaciers are melting. I gazed down this beautiful U-shaped valley, mountain peaks on the left, mountain peaks on the right. A small creek meandered through the valley, occasionally emptying into a small, crystal clear mountain lake and then on the downhill side of the small lakes the creek would continue through the beautiful green meadows and coniferous forest; eventually emptying into the very large Many Glacier Lake. We could just see the old wooden Many Glacier Lodge at the edge of the big lake. It was an absolutely beautiful scene, a gorgeous U-shaped, glacier-carved valley.

I looked at the ranger and said, "So, this glacier once filled this entire valley?"

"Yes," he said to me in his best matter-of-fact ranger voice. "Thousands of years ago this entire valley was filled by that glacier. If you look high up on the ridgeline to the east, you can see the variation of color in the rock. That's where we estimate the top of the ice reached."

"Wow, that's awesome," I said. Then I couldn't leave the conversation there, I couldn't leave well enough alone. "Gee, so the glacier started melting. And melting and melting. And eventually, it melted and retreated and exposed this beautiful glacial carved valley?"

"Yes," he replied.

I gave him a quizzical look and asked, "So, what's the problem?" He just looked at me with his eyes growing wider and wider and his lower jaw slowly dropping open. I could tell I was about to get an environmental lesson on the dangers of rising sea levels. Luckily, my pager went off. I excused myself to find a strong cell signal. The page was from the boss in Seattle.

The SAIC told me that as soon as we had a wheels-up of Air Force Two, I should get my ass to Springfield, Oregon, as quickly and safely as humanly possible. "Sure, boss, I can do that. What's up?"

The SAIC told me that a pipe bomb had been found in a drainage culvert under the driveway from the private operator side of the Springfield-Eugene Airport on the exit to the main road out of the airport area. Air Force One was scheduled to use that airport for a landing during President Clinton's visit to Springfield, Oregon, three days from now.

"All of my Portland agents are tied up with the security advances and the FBI is running wild on this one. All available Seattle agents are working with the PPD advance team here in Seattle; I have no agents available to work the investigation with them. As soon as you get to Springfield, report to the FBI resident agent in charge. You will be the Secret Service lead on this investigation until the Portland agents can take over."

When I arrived at the FBI office the next morning I went in to the boss's office and introduced myself. He was wound pretty tight. I'd say he was at about fifty thousand feet and climbing. The first thing he said to me was, "This was an assassination attempt...Wouldn't you agree this was an assassination attempt?" He was panting.

"Fill me in on what the investigation as found so far," I said, explaining that I'd been at Glacier National Park with the Vice President, and I had only sketchy information on what we had here.

I knew I was going to have to choose my words very carefully with this guy. The law is very clear on assassination attempts—the FBI has investigative jurisdiction of presidential assassination attempts; however, the Secret Service has investigative jurisdiction of threats to assassinate the President. Bottom line: jurisdictional turf war.

After he briefed me on the details, I told him, "I don't think we can make the leap, at this early stage of the investigation, that it was definitely an attempt on the life of President Clinton. We still don't know if the target of the pipe bomb was the President or if it was someone pissed off at the fixed base operator at the airport. I mean we just don't know at this point." I said, "Plus, there have been no news reports on which airport Air Force One will land. There are numerous exit points at the Eugene airport the motorcade could use. No other pipe bombs were found at the other exits from the ramp to the road. I just don't think we can say for certain it was an assassination attempt...yet."

I love to give my buddies at Freddie, Bernie, and Irving a hard time, but to be honest, the FBI is a fine organization, with some really good investigators. I was impressed with how the agents attacked this investigation. The FBI office in Springfield is small and I don't remember how many permanently assigned agents were there, but by the end of the day, they must have had close to fifty agents working this case. They had evidence technicians, surveillance technicians, criminal investigators, the whole frickin' nine yards. They scoured that town, following every lead to its end. I was impressed.

However, Freddie, Bernie and Irving just don't get it. Two days later, President Clinton stopped for his short, three-hour visit to Springfield—I don't even remember why he was there or what event or events were scheduled. I was holed up in the FBI office trying to keep the FBI boss at a breathable altitude. He was really, really nervous while President Clinton was on the ground. As we sat in the FBI office and monitored the President's motorcade from the airport, the event and motorcade back to Air Force One, the FBI agents were still out chasing down leads, and we were still trying to identify a suspect. There is one thing that has stuck with me all these years about that FBI that I learned that day: the FBI doesn't work weekends.

Once Air Force One had a wheels-up from the Springfield-Eugene airport at around four-thirty or five that Friday afternoon, the FBI boss put his feet up on his desk and for the first time in days he seemed to relax. He let out a deep breath and looked at me, "Well, what do you guys do now?" he asked me.

"What do you mean, what do we do now?" I asked him.

"Well," he said, "President Clinton is flying to Los Angeles... so this is their problem now, right?" I could not believe what I just heard him say. *Are you kidding me? Their problem?* I looked at my watch and noted it was after five o'clock on a Friday—his weekend was just getting started. "No," I said very seriously, "We *have* to find this guy. We have to conduct a through Protective Intelligence investigation on this guy or guys. We have a lot of work to do. The Secret Service will not rest until we figure out if that pipe bomb was placed in that culvert to target the life of the President. Who he is, where he is, and whether he will try it again."

About this time the Portland Secret Service boss and his three agents walked into the FBI office. The Portland boss wanted (and needed) a through briefing on the status of the investigation, five o'clock Friday or not. The FBI boss got a little defensive. "Well, all my out-of-town folks are flying back to their respective field offices tonight."

"That's no problem," said the Portland Secret Service boss. "I've got three agents, you've probably got three agents, let's get to work."

You could tell the FBI had no inclination to work on this case tonight or Saturday or God forbid, Sunday. I stepped out of the room and let the two bosses discuss this and I gave a briefing to the Portland Secret Service agent who would be handling the case.

Finally, the two bosses walked out into the main office area. The Secret Service boss was visibly upset, but he had acquiesced to the FBI boss in the spirit of "let's all get along." We paused at the door to the hallway and shook hands with the FBI boss.

"Okay, as agreed," said the Secret Service boss, directing his comments to the FBI boss and the other Portland Secret Service agents, "We'll be here Monday morning at eight to continue this investigation. Have a nice weekend." I headed back to Seattle and you can bet the Portland Secret Service office worked all weekend on that case…that's just the way we are.

* * *

In Seattle, I was the Donnie. I was the senior agent who'd done a big ugly FO and a permanent protection assignment. And yes, I too was filling my "brag sheet" with a lot of "I did this" and "I did that" bullshit, looking for a promotion to GS-14, just like my old buddy Donnie. We had some young agents right out of training and the boss had me mentoring a couple of them. One late rainy Seattle night one of the young guys calls, and wakes the Redhead and the dog…some things never change.

He'd gotten a duty call from the Blaine, Washington, Police Department and they had one in custody for passing one counterfeit twenty. Awesome! Let's roll! Working in a field office like Seattle was a pretty docile place after Vegas. We rarely got after-hours telephone calls.

I picked up the agent and we made the long drive north on Interstate 5 to the small border town of Blaine. The cops had a thirty-year-old known drug dealer in custody for passing a counterfeit twenty at a "stop and rob." This guy could have been the poster child for First Lady Nancy Reagan's "Just Say No" anti-drug campaign. His brain was completely fried, dude. Completely…fried.

The cops said he was well known up on the border as a suspected smuggler of BC Bud, a variety of marijuana grown in western Canada that was very popular in Seattle in those days. It might still be, for all I know. The cops had him primed and ready for our arrival. "The feds are coming to arrest you on a big-time counterfeiting charge. You are sunk now!"

It didn't take long to roll him…he was extremely anxious to cooperate with the Secret Service; he swore he didn't know the note was counterfeit. Dude. He didn't know. Some customer must have passed it to him when he sold the guy some dope. "Dude. I didn't have any idea it was counterfeit." And we believed him completely. That guy was so out of it, that twenty could have been Chinese and he wouldn't have known the difference. But we figured we might as well take advantage of the situation and see if we could get inside his house for a look around. The local narcs were salivating at this prospect. He was willing to execute a written consent to search. "Dude, I want to cooperate with you guys. Dude…I can't do federal time!" *Really? Awesome, let's go home, buddy.*

We conducted a search of his house and recovered so many bags of dope we were going to need a moving van to get them to the PD station. We were in the basement finishing up the consent search when the handcuffed Mr. Dude says, "Hey, man, get a screwdriver. See that third step up from the bottom? Take out the screws." Inside we found over $280,000 in US currency. The young agent and I examined every note. Every one of them. They were all genuine and they now all belonged to the Blaine PD. The duty AUSA declined to prosecute Mr. Dude for passing counterfeit and we turned him over to the Blaine PD, who were very happy to take custody of him, his dope, and his cash, and I'm sure they ended up owning the house, too.

* * *

I finally got a telephone call from the FBI technician concerning the fingerprint examination on the "Frenchman." No record. None. His fingerprints were not on file with the FBI. They assigned a new unique FBI number to Mr. Stefano. I stared at the telephone in disbelief. I could see Donnie standing at my office doorway, silently mouthing the words, "They are not who they say they are, and this isn't the first time they've done it."

This can't be right...can it? No record? None? Donnie's first rule of thumb when working a fraudster is an undeniable fact. *This guy is not Henri Stefano, no way.* I jumped on the NCIC computer—the National Crime Information Center is an outstanding computer database run by my buddies...Freddie, Bernie, and Irving. To "run" a suspect the investigator enters all the personal identifying information available on the guy, including his birthday. One unique feature is an investigator can use a range for a DOB. I figured this guy's age and started submitting requests entering different DOBs. I got pages and pages of possible hits and pored over them. One name kept coming up. Thomas Charles Edwards. Convicted of theft of mail and credit card fraud by the Postal Inspection Service in Denver, Colorado. Sentenced to three years in federal prison. There was an outstanding warrant for Edwards's arrest for escape. He'd escaped from the federal penitentiary in Florence, Colorado, about nine months prior. He obviously was not at the supermax prison in Florence, and after a little checking with Bureau of Prisons I found that there was also a minimum-security prison in Florence. I made a telephone call to the US Marshals office; they confirmed that Edwards had been incarcerated at the minimum-security prison, and one day...he just walked away.

But I still had a big problem to solve...the FBI said he was not Thomas Charles Edwards. He was Henri Stefano from frickin' France. I got on the telephone and called the Postal Inspection

Service in Denver. The duty inspector took my call. "Edwards, sure I know Edwards...I arrested him."

What luck! With one telephone call I was talking to the inspector who'd investigated, arrested, and successfully convicted Edwards. Picture? "Sure I have his picture in my file." E-mail was just getting its feet wet with Uncle Sugar and our e-mail system was not sophisticated enough to handle a scanned photo, so the Inspector faxed me a copy of Edwards's picture. A fax copy of a photo is a pretty shitty reproduction, but I could tell from the faxed photo of Edwards that he looked an awful like Stefano. "Overnight me a good copy would you?" And a couple of days later I had that two by three glossy in my hands. The Frenchman sure looked like Edwards.

I called the FBI technician right away and left a message for him to call me ricky-tick...please. And I'll be damned. They made a mistake. They compared Edwards's prints to Stefano's prints and... voilà! Same guy! To think how close this escaped federal prisoner was to completely scamming the judicial system into believing he was Henri Stefano from France is scary.

We ended up indicting Edwards on numerous counts of credit card fraud committed in the Seattle area. And then I had to deal with the suppression hearing. I knew this was going to happen and I was dreading it. I was sure we had a really good chance to lose all the evidence. You don't use a grand jury subpoena to seize this type of evidence; that's why they make search warrants, for Christ's sake! My AUSA was a little worried, too; it seems the AUSA my colleague had spoken to way back over Christmas while I was walking a golf course with Prime Minister Chrétien, had been on a one-month loan from the Social Security Administration to get some criminal experience. But by the time the case was ready for the judicial proceedings, she was long gone, back working civil cases against Grandma for cashing dead Grandpa's Social Security checks.

To obtain a search warrant an agent has to have very specific probable cause. Defense attorneys will still file a motion to suppress the search and invalidate the evidence, but rarely does the prosecution lose those hearings. *But a frickin' grand jury subpoena? Shit. If this evidence is suppressed, we ain't got much.* The hearing was touch and go; one minute you think the judge is on your side, and the next he's agreeing with the defense counsel. Fortunately, I had a squared-away AUSA on this case and she put in hours of legal research, hours she wouldn't have had to waste had we gotten a search warrant, to show the judge that case law said the seizing of the evidence was legal and the evidence should not be suppressed. We won by a squeaker, by a nose. Mr. Edwards's crime spree was halted.

Thomas Charles Edwards aka Henri Stefano went to jail for a long, long time. He was extradited to US district court in Denver to face the escape charges. The Bureau of Prisons doesn't take kindly to prisoners who escape their facilities. I'm sure Mr. Edwards did some hard time in a real federal penitentiary...one with tall walls.

And all that personal property? I had a hell of a time properly disposing of those dirty blue jeans. The King County Jail refused to take them into his jail property, the US Marshals refused to take them into their property system. I eventually got the AUSA to talk Edwards defense attorney into accepting and signing for all of it. No telling what they did with that stuff.

Chapter 15

Redemption

The Beaver seemed to be following me…while I was at PPD on President Clinton's detail; the Beaver got transferred from Las Vegas to Intelligence Division in Washington, DC, and the quest for the best cheeseburger in our nation's capital began. The Tombs in Georgetown, Ben's Chili Bowl, and of course the legendary Hawks and Doves; but it just wasn't the same as those Las Vegas dives. There is something about going to lunch in a suit and tie that ruins the experience of a good cheeseburger.

When I transferred the Redhead to Seattle after my stint at PPD, the Beaver was promoted to the resident agent in the Seattle FO's Anchorage RA. You can bet I went to Alaska at every opportunity to help the Beaver out with protection visits and criminal cases.

In February 1999 I was promoted to the Boise, Idaho, RA as the resident agent. The Boise office was under the supervision of the

Salt Lake City office of the Secret Service. I wasn't in Boise long before the Beaver was promoted to the resident agent in charge of the Salt Lake City office. Great. Now he was my boss.

* * *

There was a guy in Idaho promoting a bizarre theory that the US government, good ol' Uncle Sugar, had sold each citizen's birthright for $600,000. "Sovereign citizenship and redemption," he called it. Who the government sold this birthright to was never real clear to me, but what was clear to me was that this guy was conducting seminars all over the western United States, instructing naive, poor, and surely uneducated folks that they could "claim" this $600,000 by writing a "sight draft" against the US Treasury using their Social Security numbers as the account number. As the Beaver always said when a suspect was lying to him, "It tortures logic."

I am sure folks paid to attend his seminars, and he was a snake oil salesman and a scam artist if there ever was one. Unfortunately, six Idaho citizens were convinced they'd just hit the mother lode and decided to start buying land, homes, cars and pickup trucks with these counterfeit US Treasury "sight drafts."

A detective from the Twin Falls, Idaho, PD called me one morning to report a sixty-year old-woman, Claudia Daley, and her thirty-year-old son, Isaac Daley, had used a "Treasury sight draft" in the amount of $79,774 to buy two brand-new Dodge Ram pickups from a Twin Falls car dealership. The detective said the dealership looked at the checks and thought they were legitimate US Treasury checks, completed the sale, and let them drive off the lot with the trucks. The dealership's finance manager had taken the checks straight to the bank and was told the checks were counterfeit.

By that afternoon I was being notified of "Treasury sight drafts" being passed at other businesses, including car dealerships and a foreclosure law firm; one was even deposited by a suspect into his own checking account.

It seems a husband and wife, Jerry and Cathy Crockett, stopped by the Boise law firm processing their foreclosure on their ranch and proudly presented a "Treasury sight draft" for $125,400 to pay off their loan and stop the foreclosure. Then they went to a car dealership and bought a brand-new Chevrolet Suburban and a new Chevrolet pickup truck for $88,400. On the way out of town, headed back to his formerly foreclosed ranch, Jerry stopped at their bank's drive through (in the brand-new pickup) and deposited a "Treasury sight draft" into their joint checking account for seventy-five hundred dollars.

On the same day, the fifth and sixth suspects, another couple, Lester and Cindy Jolly bought two used cars on one "Treasury sight draft" for (only) $28,200.

All six of these folks were "Constitutionalists" fervently believing the United States government had no authority over them. They refused to comply with simple laws, like obtaining a driver's license and they refused to comply with more complex laws, like paying taxes. During the course of the investigation I'd found another common thread—they were all either heavily in debt or just plain old poor and "down on their luck" as my Dad used to say about the veterans he hired at his restaurant. All six attended one of the "Redemption" seminars and they fell for the "Redemption" tale as told by the "snake oil salesman." Money talks to everyone, even "Constitutionalists" and they all wanted "free" money from the government they insisted had no authority over them.

I presented the cases to a federal grand jury and we got a True Bill against each defendant. When a True Bill is issued by the grand jury, a US district court judge can sign an arrest warrant or issue the defendant a summons to appear in court. My AUSA wanted to have a summons issued for each defendant. In Las Vegas, T.J.

never asked for a summons to be issued; he always let us go put handcuffs on a defendant, but, what the heck, none of them had criminal records. One was actually a retired deputy sheriff from Washington State. All six lived in very rural Idaho...way out in the middle of nowhere.

However, convincing these six to comply with the legal authority granted by the US Congress to me was quite an undertaking. I took a deputy from Twin Falls County with me and we eventually found Claudia Daley in a ramshackle of an eighty-year-old house on a dirt road south of the Snake River Canyon. I don't think she even had a mailbox, much less electricity or plumbing. She was cordial, but very leery toward me. She said her son and his family lived with her, but he wasn't home. And she wouldn't tell me where he was. She kept telling me I had no authority over her, but she accepted the summons to appear in court and accepted service for her son. I kind of got the feeling that deep down inside she knew she was wrong, she knew I did have the authority to arrest her or to serve her with the summons, but in her twisted uneducated mind she was hoping "the snake oil salesman" was right about his theory of redemption.

Mr. and Mrs. Crockett were easy to find; their ranch was on a county road in south central Idaho near the Middle Fork of the Salmon River. I called the sheriff in that rural county and he said he knew them both, "Stop by my office tomorrow and I'll send my deputy who works that section of the county with you. My deputy is about the only guy that they'll halfway listen to around here."

Crockett was working in an alfalfa field on his small ranch when we drove up. "You have no authority over me," he said when he got off his tractor.

"Well, Jerry, I do; but I didn't come here to debate you. We could go on for hours and hours about my authority, and you know what, Jerry?"

"What?" he said.

"At the end of the day, I doubt I'd convince you. So let's just agree to disagree."

He took the summons for himself and his wife. I saw four youngsters running around the yard of the ranch house off in the distance. "Those kids probably don't need their mom and dad being hauled off to jail, so just do them a favor and cooperate."

He looked at the summons and I could see his lips moving as he read it. He looked up at the deputy. "Do I have to accept this?"

"Yes sir," drawled the deputy.

Jerry folded the summons and stuck it in his rear pocket. "Get off my property, you're tre-ah-spassin'."

Lester and Cindy didn't fit the mold of the other two couples. I think they had an education; Cindy was a bank teller at a local rural bank in a small town south of Boise. Lester was the retired deputy sheriff from Washington State. I pulled up to their house with a county deputy sheriff in his car. Lester was in the front yard working on his old car, the one he'd traded in the day he used the "Treasury sight draft." Unfortunately, the couple's new cars had been repossessed by the dealership.

Lester hit me with the tried old "you don't have any authority over me" line. I was done with that shit. "Lester, what the fuck is wrong with you?" I asked him. "If anybody should know better, it's you. You're a retired deputy sheriff, for Christ's sake. You know damn well I have authority over you and you know damn well I have the authority to come on your property to serve you with this summons." I handed him the papers. "I'll see you in court, pal."

When Claudia and her son showed up at their initial appearance before the US magistrate judge, they refused to cooperate with the court, refused to be interviewed by pretrial services, refused to fill out the financial affidavit, and refused the services of the federal public defender. "Are you Claudia Daley and are you Isaac Daley?" the judge asked them.

Claudia stood up. "My name is my business," she said. "You have no authority over me." *Oh, boy. Here we go; this is going to be a real circus.* She continued, "I was served these papers," she said as she held up the summons, "by a foreign agent who did not have authority to enter my private property. We are here solely for a visitation and nothing more."

That snake oil salesman must be dishing out legal advice at his seminars, too.

Eventually, the magistrate proceeded with the initial appearance, with or without their participation. He released them on a five-thousand-dollar unsecured bond. All they had to do was sign the judge's order of their release conditions and come back to court for the next court hearing. But no; they refused to sign anything, Claudia muttering something about a "straw man" that I didn't catch. I'd quit listening to her ramblings ten minutes into the hearing.

The magistrate Judge had had enough. He banged the gavel and I started paying attention. "Mrs. Daley, if you or Isaac refuse to sign that document, I will order the US Marshal to take you into custody and both of you will sit in a jail cell until trial."

I looked at Claudia, I could see that same look on her face as when I served her the summons, and I could read her mind. She was thinking, *maybe he does have the authority, maybe we should sign this document.*

She huddled with Isaac and then said, "We will sign under objection and without accepting the jurisdiction of the court."

The initial appearances for the other four defendants all followed the same script before the magistrate. Jerry and Cathy eventually signed the conditions of release, but with the exact same speech to the judge. Lester, the retired deputy sheriff, flatly refused to sign his release documents. Cindy following his led and also refused. The US Marshals handcuffed them and led them out of the courtroom to the lockup. I walked back to the lockup with a deputy US Marshal. Lester was standing in the holding cell, I guess I felt sorry for the dumb ass, I guess the fact he was a retired cop played on my emotions. Whatever the reason, I walked over to his cell and said, "Lester, if you sign the release conditions form for the judge, you can go home. Don't be a fool."

He changed his mind and we called the magistrate. I was starting to think he had some sense and then he launched into the judge with the same—the exact same—words as Claudia had used. That snake oil salesman must have been a pretty convincing teacher, and I was sorry I'd wasted my time trying to talk some sense into him.

Needless to say all six defendants took their case to trial and a jury convicted all six. Each trial was a complete circus, with the defendants refusing to address the court and constantly challenging the authority of the proceedings. It wasn't as bad as the Jeff Hunt counterfeiting trial in Las Vegas, but it was close.

All six went to prison. Claudia and Isaac only got six months, and four years' probation; Jerry Crockett was sentenced to eighteen months in prison and three years' probation; Cathy Crockett got twelve months and three years' probation. Cindy Jolly got ten months and three years' probation. The US district court judge thought Lester, the retired deputy sheriff, should have known better; Lester was sentenced to twenty-four months in prison and four years' probation.

* * *

I didn't stay in Boise long. In February 2001 I was promoted to a GS-14 on PPD...back to the East Coast we went. The Redhead is a trouper when it came to my career. Even though she hated the East Coast as much as Las Vegas, she agreed we could make that move. I just had to promise her we wouldn't stay there for too long; she had to get back to the west coast before this adventure with me was over. "No problem," I told her. "When have I been afraid of moving?"

And we didn't stay long. Eighteen months later we were moving once again. A relocation list had been published in the late spring of 2002 and the assistant special agent in charge position was open at the Seattle Field Office. I'd only been at PPD for a little over one year, in my mind there was no way I would be selected for that promotion—but, I'd promised the Redhead we'd go back to the west coast as soon as possible.

I was shocked when the list came out and I was promoted to the ASAIC in Seattle. I guess nobody else put in for it, because to get transferred out of DC in less than two years was very, very rare. By the time we sold the house and packed up for Seattle only eighteen months had gone by. Twenty-four months in Boise and eighteen months back in DC, three moves in three and one-half years.

On the morning of our second day on the road trip from Virginia to Seattle, the Redhead picked up a newspaper in the lobby of our hotel for something to read while I drove. "There's an article in here about Putin and they printed that old photo of President Bush driving Putin around his Texas ranch in your truck!" She held the newspaper up for me to take a look.

"I'll be darned," I said. "My truck is famous!"

During my short assignment as a GS-14 on PPD, George W. Bush was President, and with my experience in the Transportation Section during my first tour of duty with President Clinton, the SAIC assigned me as the supervisor of TS.

It wasn't long after 9-11 and President Bush was scheduled to visit his ranch in Waco, Texas. He'd been in the market for a new Ford F-150 pickup truck and he just hadn't had the time to go car shopping; so the Secret Service decided to buy one for his use.

Early one Saturday morning I got a telephone call at my residence from the SAIC. He told me to go buy the President a pickup. And to do it today. *Okay, I can do that.* And then he told me to get it to Detroit by Sunday night, so the small manufacturing plant where our new Beasts were being assembled could complete some security upgrades on the vehicle before we transported it to Waco the next weekend. *Ohhh-kay. Aye, aye, sir.*

The bureaucracy of the government is notoriously s-l-o-w. But let me tell you something…when the President of the United States needs something, that bureaucracy can move pretty fast. The boss gave me a telephone number of a big shot at the General Service Administration (GSA) and instructed me on the details of the F-150 (color, interior, options, etc.).

I told Mr. Big from GSA what I needed. He called me back in about an hour. The only F-150 that met "my" specifications was at a dealership in Jefferson City, Missouri. "Buy it," I said. "Right now. And get it delivered to Detroit by Sunday afternoon." GSA wired the dealer the money and GSA contracted a local flatbed tow truck driver to go get it and deliver it to "my" address outside Detroit, Michigan. His instructions were to have it in Detroit by six o'clock Sunday evening.

I kissed the Redhead good-bye, told her I'd see her when I see her, and drove to Dulles Airport to catch the next commercial flight to Detroit. One of the PPD ASAICs and one of the best mechanical technicians employed by the Secret Service's Special Services Division (SSD) were going with me to Detroit. As a matter of fact this tech was the brains behind the design of the Beast. He was good.

I was late for my flight, and there is nothing that gets my goat like being late for a flight. Air traffic had recently been opened up again after 9-11 and Dulles Airport was chaos. All the long-term parking lots were full. Every one of them and believe me, I drove up and down each aisle of each lot. Not a single open parking space.

I had to get going, so I parked my G-ride in the daily parking (expensive) lot. I figured I'd deal with that later, and boy did I... Uncle Sugar will only reimburse a federal worker so much for airport parking and my cheap-ass uncle made me eat the bill, emergency or no emergency.

TSA hadn't yet been born at this early stage after 9-11 and the contract airport security companies were still trying to come to grips with new security requirements, as were passengers. The terminal at Dulles was packed with people. When I came into the ticketing terminal I could not believe how many folks were crammed into line at the ticket counter. I searched for the end of a long line of travelers from the west entrance door all the way down to the United Airlines ticket counter at the east end of the terminal. *Jesus! That is the line for United Airlines ticketing?* So I walked back to the end and shuffled along with the rest of the anxious travelers.

Fortunately, all of the flights that day were extremely late and I boarded my flight with my two cohorts. The next day, Sunday morning, bright and early we drove our rental car from our hotel to the very non-descript building in an industrial park in Detroit to wait for the pickup to arrive that evening. We discussed our security requirements for the F-150 with the very small crew that was building our Beasts. They planned to get to work on the F-150 at six o'clock that evening and have it finished on Monday. Beast number four was in production (as in being hand assembled by these expert craftsman) and Beast number five was just a chassis sitting there and waiting to be next. To meet their delivery time line on number four, they had to get the pickup done before noon Monday; eighteen hours from the time they received the vehicle.

They gave us a tour of their small plant. I learned a tremendous amount about the Beast that day, all the ins and outs of the security features, that I already knew about and how to operate; but during this briefing I learned how they were designed and constructed. That alone made the trip worthwhile.

As the day wore on and we were basically twiddling our thumbs, the manager/owner/head engineer asked if I'd like to sign the roof of number four. "What do you mean sign the roof?" I asked him. He told me they would be honored if I autographed the roof before they assembled the outer layer.

I guess they thought I was a big shot...*geez; I'm just a GS-14 who supervises the PPD Transportation Section, but, what the heck! They think I'm important enough to autograph the roof of Beast number four, then shit, give me a pen!* And so I did. I put a *big* signature on the roof and added "ATSAIC PPD Transportation" with the date. Awesome!

We still had some time to kill, waiting for the tow truck driver to show up, so the plant boss said they needed to do a test drive on number four with a laptop plugged into the intricate electronic onboard systems. One of the engineers hooked up his laptop, we all piled in and off we went down the freeways of Detroit with yours truly behind the wheel. So I can safely say, I was the first agent to drive number four. Coupled with my autograph on the roof, I'd say that Beast is my baby!

Six o'clock rolled around and no flatbed tow truck with "my" pickup. We called the driver's cell phone. No answer. Seven o'clock, no truck. At about 8 o'clock we started making telephone calls to the tow truck business. On a Sunday night. Do you know how hard it is to track down the telephone numbers of people on a Sunday night? It is not easy. We had a cell phone number for the driver, but he was not answering. We called the transport company...no answer. Of course, it's Sunday night and they are closed. At about midnight Monday morning we finally got someone on the phone from the transport company. And they didn't know shit. The driver was instructed to be in Detroit by six Sunday evening. They don't know where he is and they have also tried calling his cellphone.

"Okay," I asked, "So what's his address?"

"Well, I don't know if I can give that kind of personal information out." *Really?*

The Secret Service tech got on the line and made a few references to National Security and high importance of that F-150 being in Detroit immediately, and lo and behold, they gave us his address.

It was getting close to one o'clock Monday morning and we had to find that driver. The Secret Service technician made a telephone call to a local sheriff's office in the county where he lived. "Would you mind sending a deputy to drive by his house and report back to us if there is a flatbed tow truck with a white F-150 Ford pickup on the back?"

"Sure. We can do that," replied the watch commander. Thirty minutes later we got a call from a deputy.

"Yes sir," he said, "I'm sitting out here on Pole Cat Road and I can see a flatbed tow truck parked next to a mobile home. There's a F-150, looks brand-new, sittin' on the back."

"Would you mind knocking on the door and handing your cell phone to Mr. Transport Driver?"

"I'd love to," said the deputy.

Mr. Transport Driver was in total shock…"Well yeah, I know I was supposed to be in Dee-Troit at six this evenin', but my back's hurtin' so I was going to get to the chiropractor first thing Monday morning and then head to Dee-Troit."

Unacceptable. In no uncertain terms the tech told him, "No. You will get in your tow truck and be in Detroit by ten o'clock this morning." He showed up at nine forty-five Monday morning with "my" truck. And he looked scared shitless. He kept muttering something about the CIA as he unloaded the F-150 from the back of his flatbed truck. His hands shook. He stuttered a little. The tech signed for the delivery and we sent him on his way. You know, I can picture Mr. Transport Driver sitting in a local hangout, nursing a beer, and muttering stories about "the day the CIA got me out of bed at one in the morning to deliver a Ford F-150 pickup truck to a nondescript building in an industrial area outside Dee-Troit, Michigan," and his buddies rolling their eyes, saying, "There he goes again, with those crazy CIA stories."

The Beast team got started on the F-150 and I was amazed at how fast they dismantled that pickup. They did the requested security upgrades and finished putting the damn thing back together again just past midnight Tuesday morning…less than fourteen hours after the truck was off-loaded. And no one ever, would be able to tell it wasn't factory. These guys were awesome.

It was time to head back to Washington, DC, and I really wanted to drive that truck back, but it's hell being a supervisor sometimes. I had to get back to DC Tuesday morning and left the transport to the SSD tech. When I got to my office, I contacted our administrative assistant in Operations and told her to make sure she registered the truck in Texas; Washington, DC, license plates probably wouldn't cut the mustard with the President.

We had the pickup scheduled for transported by the air force to Waco on Friday afternoon and President Bush had yet to lay eyes on it. The SAIC called me Thursday morning and said to bring the F-150 over to the White House ASAP; the President wanted to take a look at it. That sounded like a job for a supervisor! So I went down to the super secret garage, jumped in the pickup and drove it over to West Executive Boulevard

The Deputy Chief of Staff came out to look her over and said he was positive President Bush would love it. Unfortunately, the President was too busy to come take a look at it that day. It was just a few weeks after 9-11 and he had other pressing matters to attend to.

Years later President Bush auctioned off his F-150 for charity. This was not the same F-150 I bought back in September 2001. President Bush had purchased another F-150 in 2009 after he left office. The F-150 I bought was a Secret Service vehicle, and if the Secret Service in Waco is not driving it, I'm sure it was sold at a GSA auction, like all used government vehicles. The big question is—*if* it was sold at auction, do you think the current owner has any idea it was once driven by the President of the United States?

Chapter 16

The Supreme Court of the United States

I reported for duty as the ASAIC in Seattle in August 2002 and settled into a desk job, supervising agents. Seattle was considered a "medium" sized office with roughly nine to eleven agents. It was good to be back in Seattle. The Redhead and I knew the area well from my first tour there after I left PPD in 1997. We even bought a house close to our old neighborhood and my old fly fishing buddy was still living down the road.

Most, if not all the agents I'd worked with during my first tour in Seattle were retired or had transferred to other assignments, so it was like being in a new office. Even the SAIC was a different person. The only constant was the office manager. Most of the agents assigned to the office were fresh from training, after having been brought onboard during a big hiring push back in 2000 and 2001. I'd look into their young faces and see myself, back in my Vegas days working with Donnie and Beaver.

The SAIC placed me in charge of supervision of all protection in the Seattle district. I made the assignments for conducting advances for visits of Secret Service protected persons who visited Seattle, made rotating rosters of Seattle agents available for protective operations travel in support of the Secret Service's world-wide protective mission and I acted as the Field Office Supervisor for all protection in the district.

Every time the President or Vice President made a trip outside of Washington, DC, those details would send agents to the local field office to conduct the security advances. The agents in the field office would be assigned to assist those agents in their security preparations. As the field office supervisor, my main responsibility was to supervise the security preparations for final approval by one of the detail's supervisors, who would typically arrive in the city in question a day or two before the visits by the President or Vice President.

My goal was always to make sure the advance agents had done a superb job on their venues and motorcades so that when the detail supervisor showed up, he would agree to their plans. I conducted a lot of security advances for the President in my PPD days and believe me, the Secret Service lead advance and the Secret Service site agents don't need their plan to change one day before the President shows up. That'll just put them behind the eight ball, scrambling at the last minute to make security changes the detail supervisor wants changed. But these individual agents are very good and I'd venture to say 97 percent of the time, I didn't need to change anything.

One of my favorite flight instructors back in my flight school days in Pensacola, Florida was a marine captain. He once told me he loved the Marine Corps, because "10 percent of the general population is fucked up, but only 3 percent of marines are fucked up." The same holds true for the Secret Service. The only problem with that theory is that if you get too many of the 3 percent in the same place at the same time…things can get fucked up real quick (i.e., Cartagena, Colombia). But, that's just my opinion.

August and September were always the two busiest months for a field office. In August all the politicians, including the President and Vice President, leave Washington, DC, for the summer recess. August has become the de facto vacation month, not only for current presidents, but former presidents as well. September is the annual head of state meetings at the United Nations in New York, thus all those Foreign Heads of State are afforded protection by the Secret Service, and believe me, September is one busy month for the Secret Service field offices. I used to tell all my young agents to forget about a personal life in August and September—and whatever you do, do not get married in August or September and for Pete's sake don't "kadoodle" with the wife in December or January because when your child is born in August or September you can plan on missing a lot of birthdays.

During my tenure as the Seattle ASAIC, for some unknown reason, presidents, vice presidents and former presidents always seemed to vacation in Seattle's geographical jurisdiction. Consequently, I had some really nice trips in those days as the field office supervisor, especially for an outdoorsy guy like me.

One summer, former president George H. W. Bush took a fishing vacation at Lake Illimani, Alaska. We only had two agents assigned to the Anchorage RA in those days so I went up there to help them out. It turned out to be a great week in the Alaskan wilderness. One of the Anchorage agents stayed in Anchorage to provide the security advance for the airport arrival and departure. The other Anchorage agent and I went to Lake Illimani to make security preparations for the former President's fishing trip.

Former President George H.W. Bush's fishing buddies on this trip included a close friend from Houston and retired air force General Chuck Yeager. Yes…that Chuck Yeager…the first man to break the speed of sound in a jet aircraft. For an old Marine A6 Bombardier/Navigator it was a thrill to meet and speak with him.

The Anchorage agent and I flew into Lake Illimani Airport on an Alaskan Airlines 737. *Great…with 737 air service this place must not be as remote as it looks on the map.* When the wheels of that 737 hit the runaway, I almost jumped out of my skin. The runway was gravel and the noise from the gravel flying off the landing gear was deafening. *Holy shit, a little gravel in one of those engines and this plane will be unflyable for weeks.* Believe me, gravel was flying everywhere. I looked at the Anchorage agent and he said to me, "We're in the middle of nowhere now, boss." And he was right; but the middle of nowhere in Alaska is breathtakingly beautiful. "If we survive the landing and takeoff from this gravel runway." I said, "This could be a good trip!"

Once we got checked into our "bunkhouse" we set out trying to find two SUVs we could rent to stand in for a limo and Secret Service follow-up. My agent from Anchorage had been in contact with the manager of the exclusive lodge where the fishing party would be staying and he was assured we could use one of their SUVs as a limo. The manager said we shouldn't have any problem "renting" another SUV from one of the other lodges in Lake Illimani. Of course, Murphy's Law always applies to a protection advance and we no sooner got to the lodge when we discovered their one and only SUV was a ten-year-old Chevy Suburban with a rear window stuck in the down position. But no problem, it runs and it'll have to do

For our Secret Service vehicle we could find only one other SUV, which an outfitter was willing to "rent" out for the week, in the small village. You guessed it; it was even older and in worse shape. We had to jump start the engine with jumper cables every time we wanted to go someplace. The outfitter told us they had a new battery on order from Anchorage and it just hadn't made it in yet. That's life in rural Alaska.

None of this was really an issue, we only needed the SUVs for the drive to and from the airport on the arrival day and the departure day about five days later; however, our evacuation plan was to get the former President to the airport if there was a medical emergency or for any other emergency that required us to get him out of Lake Illimani. God knows there was only one dirt road through the village, so there weren't many places to drive.

Every morning during his stay, former president Bush, his Houston buddy, and Chuck Yeager would load up on a floatplane and fly into the wilderness for some serious all-day fishing. The former president's detail supervisor went with them in the small floatplane and we, of course, stayed back in the village to stand by with our satellite telephone in case there was an emergency and they needed to get back to civilization.

We didn't have much to do all day in the village, so one day the outfitter at our bunkhouse lodge offered to take us salmon fishing in his jet boat up the Newhalen River, which flows into Lake Illimani. It didn't take too long out on that river to understand why he had that type of boat. The river is more than a quarter of a mile wide where it dumps into the lake, but only about eighteen inches deep. With a very, very swift current. A jet boat is about the only thing that can traverse that shallow of water.

After we got a few miles upstream, the river narrowed to a more normal width for a mountain river and was choked full of rapids. The river curved through a canyon dotted with boulders as big as a house. That was one fun ride up (and down) that river.

"This is what we call 'the slot' boys," he told us. "This is where we fish." Millions of king salmon, and I mean millions, were "holding" in the pool under the last rapids; rapids so intense even the jet boat could go no further upriver. But not the salmon, they were resting up for the dash upstream to their spawning beds. It looked like you could walk across the river by stepping on salmon and you would not get your feet wet. Needless to say, I caught a ton of big king salmon that day. It was almost too easy.

That wasn't the only fishing trip I took with a former President as the ASAIC in Seattle. Former president Carter went fishing on the Kenai River in Alaska one summer and I again was able to work in a day of fishing for trout. The Redhead always enjoyed these trips to Alaska…I was able to stock our freezer with some delicious salmon and trout.

Not all the good deals were in Alaska, either. One July day I got a telephone call from the headquarters Protection Operations agent. This agent was respectfully referred to as the "body snatcher." Every month I had a quota to fill with headquarters, providing them the names of agents in the Seattle District (Seattle, Portland, Spokane, Great Falls, and Anchorage) who were available to travel in support of our protective mission during the upcoming month. As soon as I answered the phone, I figured he needed more agents for the August assignments. But no. He needed me. "Hey!" he said, "do you have any plans the last three weeks of July? Would you like to go to the French Riviera with Nancy Reagan?"

Would I like to go to the French Rivera? With my favorite cookie baker? I don't even have to call the Redhead on this one, because I'm going with or without her blessing. Sometimes you've just got to do what the job requires!

The Secret Service has a field office in Paris to cover parts of Europe. It seemed the Paris field office had too many protection visits at one time and not enough agents to cover Nancy Reagan. They needed a field office supervisor and I was the man for the job. Mrs. Reagan and two girlfriends were planning on cruising the southern French coastline for fifteen days on a private yacht. I spent almost three full weeks on the French southern coast and I saw Mrs. Reagan three times. Once when we picked her up at the airport in Nice and motorcaded her to the yacht. The second time when she docked at Saint Tropez and we took her to Merv Griffin's yacht for dinner. And the last time when the cruise was over and we motorcaded her from the boat dock to the Nice airport. Let me tell you, that was one nice trip to Nice. I saw the entire southern coast of France, got to explore Saint Tropez and live a bit of the high life.

But in Seattle I had even better trips with First Lady Laura Bush.

In July 2003 First Lady Laura Bush was planning a camping and hiking trip to Glacier National Park, Montana. I made the long drive in my G-ride to the Park headquarters to meet up with the PPD First Lady's detail and review the security plan they had put together. Unfortunately, that year wildfires were consuming the park, and as I drove into Glacier National Park, I could see and smell the smoke from the still out-of-control fire.

The park superintendent had strongly recommended that Mrs. Bush and her party cancel the trip. Prior to traveling to Glacier, I had seen the news reports on the wildfire, and in the back of my mind I'd thought maybe she would have to cancel the trip. But until you see the massive destruction a wildfire can do, up close and personal, and you smell the smoke and see the flames: well, once I witnessed the fire, it was a no-brainer; she had to cancel.

Canceling a trip is not an easy task. Convincing the SAIC of PPD that this visit to the park was a really bad idea was the easy part. Convincing the White House staff that it was a bad idea to take camping and hiking vacation to Glacier National Park—a vacation the First Lady had planned for over one year—well, that was the hard part. It seemed like we were on the telephone for hours with Mrs. Bush's staff before they finally got it. The park was being consumed by a wildfire, and there was no place to camp or hike without being in danger. One change in the wind direction and you could be in harm's way.

For Mrs. Bush and her friends, changing those plans would result in a big disappointment. And since the plans had centered around the First Lady of the United States, that just made the decision that much more difficult—Secret Service agents had to conduct a security advance, logistics had to be ironed out, and emergency plans developed.

A few hours later, the staff contacted the PPD First Lady's detail lead advance agent. Glacier National Park, eight to nine hours by G-ride east of Seattle, was canceled. However, the vacation would go as scheduled in Olympic National Park, three or fours hours west of Seattle, with no change to her arrival date.

Early the next morning the advance team hopped a commercial airline for Seattle, and yours truly hit the road in his G-ride for the twelve- or thirteen-hour drive to Olympic National Park.

The First Lady's visit to Olympic National Park was a great success, but due to the last-minute change in location, the vacationers had to stay in a hotel instead of camping in the backcountry. The weather was perfect during their visit and the scenery in the park was spectacular. All in all, they seemed to really enjoy their visit.

When 2004 rolled around, I was hoping Mrs. Bush and her friends would return for their summer vacation to Glacier National Park, and I wasn't disappointed.

In late July 2004, in the mist of a presidential reelection campaign, Mrs. Bush and her lady friends arrived in Glacier National Park. We backpacked to a backcountry campground and Ranger Station and set up camp. We accompanied the ladies every morning on their day hikes around the park, and in the evenings we sat around the campfire after dinner with them.

Mrs. Bush and her friends were some of the nicest people you could meet. We had a great time sitting around the campfire in the

evenings and telling stories. One night, Mrs. Bush was telling us
about some of the parks she and her friends had visited in the past
and they were discussing future trips for inclusion in their quest to
hike them all.

"Mrs. Bush," I said to her, "have you been to Denali National
Park in Alaska?"

"No," she replied. "Have you been there?"

In the summer of 2003, the Redhead and I had taken a vacation
to Denali National Park and the unspoiled beauty of Denali
enthralled us. Denali is a huge park, but it only has one road. A dirt
road ninety-three miles from the park entrance to the old mining
town of Kantishna, Alaska.

No private cars are allowed in the park, but the Park Service
has a vendor to take tourists down the ninety-three-mile dirt road
to the town of Kantishna. The Redhead and I saw numerous grizzly
bears, herds and herds of caribou and moose, all from the safety of a
large converted school bus. We watched a grizzly bear stalk, pounce
upon, kill, and devour a beaver—it was a National Geographic
moment!

"Denali sounds wonderful," she said to me. "We'll have to give
that some consideration."

* * *

As the presidential campaign rolled toward the 2004 November
election, the President was on a final West Coast campaign swing
in mid-October and his reelection team scheduled a two-day visit
to Medford, Oregon, with a huge rally planned at the Medford
fairgrounds.

Mrs. Bush had had a separate campaign itinerary and she would
arrive at the Medford airport minutes before Air Force One, where
she would join the President for the Medford, Oregon, campaign

rally. On arrival day, Mrs. Bush and her entourage arrived as scheduled a few minutes before Air Force One.

Upon the arrival of Mrs. Bush, some of her staff deplaned, while she waited on board for the President. I saw her military doctor deplane and he walked over to say hello to me. We shot the breeze for the bit and then he said, "I haven't seen you since we were in Glacier National Park last July. We were just talking about you on the flight into Medford!"

"Really?" I said. I started to asked him about the conversation when he was called over by one of the staff.

"I have to go," he said and shook my hand. "It was nice seeing you again, take care of yourself."

The PPD First Lady's detail leader walked out of the First Lady's aircraft and walked over to me to say hello. "Good to see you again," he said. "Mrs. Bush was just talking about you on the airplane as we flew into Medford."

"No kidding," I said, "what's that all about?"

"She was discussing next summer's hiking trip, trying to pinpoint a destination," he told me, "and she said Tim wants to go to Denali, so let's plan on that for the summer of 2006!"

Air Force One was on final approach to the Medford airport ending the conversation. But I had to smile—Denali! That's going to be one great hiking trip with Mrs. Bush.

* * *

The staff decided to have the President and Mrs. Bush spent the night at the Jacksonville Inn and Cottages, located in the old gold mining town of Jacksonville, Oregon, five miles west of Medford. In 1966, downtown Jacksonville was designated a US National Historic Landmark. It is a picturesque western town.

The main street bisecting Jacksonville from east to west is California Street. The main inn and restaurant are located on the north side of California Street and the cottages are tucked behind the storefronts on the south side of California Street. The PPD advance team set up a secure perimeter around the city block south of California Street to ensure the safety of the President and Mrs. Bush—standard operating procedure for a presidential stay in a hotel. California Street marked the northern perimeter of the secure area and was left open for pedestrian and vehicular traffic, as were all the small businesses lining downtown Jacksonville.

We motorcaded the President and Mrs. Bush to the campaign rally and at the conclusion of that event, we motorcaded directly to the Jacksonville Inn to spend the night. When we were a few minutes away from arriving at the Inn, I heard on my Secret Service Motorola radio that President and Mrs. Bush were going to make an "off the record" stop for dinner at the Jacksonville Inn restaurant.

A presidential motorcade has many, many vehicles to carry the traveling party, comprised of White House staff, campaign staff, military personnel, Secret Service agents and the press corps. It is not unusual to have thirty cars or minivans in the motorcade. The arrival area, in a narrow alley east of the Inn, had room for the presidential limo and the Secret Service follow-up. The motorcade advance agent had the rest of the motorcade break off and park behind the Inn to the north.

By the time I made my way from my vehicle to the Jacksonville Inn, the President, Mrs. Bush and their staff were already in the restaurant. As I approached the limo, at the side door to the restaurant I could see California Street was packed full of Iraq war protesters. Most, if not all, had bandanas covering their faces; they appeared young and extremely angry. The scene reminded me of the protesters in Seattle at the World Trade Organization meeting in November of 1999.

The protesters were within feet of the presidential limo. I was told President and Mrs. Bush were seated in an outdoor patio dining area, behind the restaurant. I looked to my right and saw that a six- to seven-foot old, worn-out wooden wall was, the only barrier between the President of the United States and about three hundred very angry Americans. I remember thinking, "Oh shit. An assassin could easily throw a hand grenade from the street right into the patio dining area."

Protests groups can turn into an uncontrollable mob in an instant. If the protesters were to get out of control, they could easily rush the patio area. And to make things worse, the protesters provided perfect cover for an assassin, someone who wasn't at the scene to protest the war, but who was there to kill the President of the United States. This was a very dangerous situation.

Of course, the PPD supervisors with the President and the lead advance agent knew exactly what I knew and long before I arrived at the alley had already directed the police to move the protesters down the street to the east a couple of blocks. By moving them the one to two blocks east, we would mitigate the threat of handgun, thrown bomb, or Molotov cocktail. Moving them would place two-story brick buildings between them and the outdoor patio, blocking the line of sight to the President and First lady.

The United States Secret Service has the legal authority, by federal statute, to secure a building for safety of the President. And, of course, Americans have the first amendment right to voice their displeasure with the policies of their government.

The police formed a line at the west end of California Street and ordered the protesters to move east two blocks. The protesters ignored the order. The police continued telling the protesters to move. The protesters continued to ignore the police commands.

Finally, a line of riot-gear-clad officers began moving down the street, forcing the protesters away from the front of the restaurant and the alley. Tear gas was deployed; many protesters sat in the street in defiance of the order to move. Those protesters had to be physically removed. It became an ugly scene, but finally the police got the crowd of protesters to a safe distance. They continued their chants protesting the Iraq war and I could plainly hear them, their voices echoing off the brick buildings that surrounded the downtown area.

The President, Mrs. Bush, and their party were still dining on the patio, but the protesters, I assume, thought by now the President had returned to his cottage and they dispersed on their own. The street was eerily quiet. I walked out to the front of the restaurant and looked up and down the street. It was empty, with just a few police officers on California Street in front of the Inn.

The remainder of the night was calm and the next morning the President and Mrs. Bush departed the Medford, Oregon, airport without incident, for the next campaign stop before the election.

A few months later the chief of the Jacksonville, Oregon, Police Department called me. He was at fifty thousand feet and climbing. He said the leader of the Jacksonville Iraq war protest had stopped by his office and was going to sue him for moving the group down California Street that night back in October.

"No shit," I calmly said. "Don't worry about lawsuits. If they sue the Jacksonville Police Department they will sue the Secret Service. You were acting at our direction and we have the legal authority to secure a venue for the President's safety. Don't sweat it. Let them sue. Any lawsuit they file will be dismissed."

And I repeated, "The United States Secret Service has the *legal* authority to secure a building for the safety of the President of the United States. It is that simple."

* * *

As the summer of 2006 approached, I was looking forward to Mrs. Bush's vacation in Denali National Park. I just hoped she and her girlfriends would enjoy it as much as the Redhead and I had three years prior; after all, apparently the vacation had been scheduled at my insistence!

I had over twenty-two years in the Secret Service that summer and I was rapidly approaching the mandatory retirement age of fifty-seven. One thing I knew for sure was that I wanted to continue working; fifty-seven is way too early an age to sit in a rocking chair, and I didn't want to be behind the eight ball with finding a second career, so I started the process of looking for a civilian job.

Just like back in 1976 when I sat on the grass outside the Memorial Union at the University of Missouri, I needed a plan. What I didn't want to happen was for me to procrastinate too long in the job search; I had nightmares of me walking into my ASAIC office on my fifty-seventh birthday and HQ calling me. "Why are you here today," I dreamed, "What? You thought the mandatory retirement age didn't apply to you? Turn in your badge and gun. And have a nice day!"

I wanted something fun and exciting to work at; after all, since college, I'd been a Marine Corps officer, a bombardier/navigator in the A6E Intruder, and then a Secret Service agent. My entire career had been an adventure...Nine to five was not going to cut it, post-USSS.

One day in May or June of 2006, I saw a job posting for a position as the director of security operations for a nonprofit organization. It sounded like a perfect fit for me, so I e-mailed them my résumé.

In July 2006 Mrs. Bush and her girlfriends came to Denali and I was in Fairbanks, Alaska, awaiting their arrival. I had just walked into my hotel room and set my bags down when my cellphone rang. It was the human resources director of this civilian outfit. "Sure," I said as I set my bags on the hotel room floor. " I've got a few minutes to speak with you right now."

The HR director finished up our telephone interview by asking me if I could fly to their headquarters next week for an interview. "Well, I'm sorry but I am currently in Alaska with the First Lady and I won't be home to Seattle for about ten days. And then I have some commitments in Seattle. Unfortunately, I won't be available for about three weeks."

To my surprise, she asked me to call her as soon as I got back to Seattle and could pinpoint a day for the in person interview. *Wow,* I thought, *things are moving real fast on this civilian job search.*

Mrs. Bush and her girlfriends arrived at the Fairbanks airport and we took them on the Alaska Railroad from Fairbanks to the Denali Park entrance. The National Park Service gave us permission to drive a small motorcade of three Secret Service vehicles into the park and down the dirt road to Kantishna and we checked into one of the private lodges at the end of the road.

For the next week, Mrs. Bush and her friends hiked on trails in the park and we took them on some animal sightseeing excursions, with the Majestic Mount McKinley as a backdrop. I didn't ask, but it seemed to me they thoroughly enjoyed Denali National Park. As Mrs. Bush got on the air force plane that would take her back to Washington, DC, I figured that was my last hiking vacation with her. And it was, because in a few weeks I would be retiring from the Secret Service.

I got back to Seattle and made the trip for the in-person interview and was offered the job. *Holy shit,* I thought, *now I have to submit my retirement papers.*

I was sitting in my office in Seattle with the August 31, 2006, retirement date rapidly closing in. My desk telephone rang. It was headquarters, The US Secret Service Legal Division. That is never a good phone call. "Are you aware of the lawsuit filed against you in US District Court, Portland, Oregon?"

What? "No," I said as I searched my memory banks for anything I did that would result in a lawsuit. "Well," she told me, "the ACLU of Oregon has filed a lawsuit surrounding the events in Jacksonville, Oregon, back in 2004"...her voice faded away in my head. The Iraq war protesters! Now I remembered the conversation with the chief of the Jacksonville Police Department over two years ago. I starting listening again, "And," she said, "they have named you, personally and individually, in the lawsuit."

I cut her off, "What does that mean?" I asked. "Well, they have named you and the PPD lead advance agent as individuals in the lawsuit and the Secret Service as an organization. That means you are being sued. Legally, it means you are being sued for damages and you are liable. But don't worry, even if in the remote possibility you lost, the federal government would cover any monetary responsibility you incur as you were acting in your official capacity when the events occurred."

Great...the Redhead is going to love this news!

She continued, "A US Justice Department attorney from the Civil Rights Division will be calling you this afternoon to discuss this case with you and give you the details of the lawsuit."

Even though I knew the lawsuit would eventually be dismissed, finding out that I was named as an individual in this lawsuit was a bit discerning. Especially since I was not involved with any of the decisions to have the police clear the street—but for the record, had I been the agent responsible for making that call, I absolutely would have ordered the police to move those protesters. That was a one of the most dangerous situations I'd ever seen for a President.

The Justice Department attorney called me and gave me a very thorough briefing on the case and the first thing he asked me was if I wanted the Justice Department attorneys to represent me, at no cost to me since I was acting in my Official capacity as an employee of the Secret Service during the day in question. One thing I learned back in my Las Vegas days was that US Justice Department career attorneys are very good. T.J. and all those AUSAs I worked criminal cases with were all career Justice Department attorneys.

The wheels of justice spin extremely slow for a civil case filed in US district court and this case would drag on and on from that early August day in 2006, when I was first notified of the lawsuit, until the final decision was handed down on May 27, 2014.

The Justice Department filed my (our) response to the plaintiffs' allegations and the US district court judge in Portland ruled against us.

We appealed his decision to the 9th Circuit Court of Appeals in San Francisco. A three-judge panel eventually heard the arguments for the lawsuit and ruled in our favor, dismissing the lawsuit; saying the plaintiffs failed to show their First Amendment right to free speech did not meet the threshold for harm. However, the 9th Circuit Court judges ruled the plaintiffs in the case should have the opportunity to refile their First Amendment claim of harm if they could better articulate their claim to conform with current case law.

Really? Really. So they started all over again with a new lawsuit. Once again, the US district court judge ruled against us, the case could go forward. We appealed to the 9th Circuit once again. This time a different three-judge panel decided the case against us. The lawsuit can move forward. We (myself and the other Secret Service agent) were *not* entitled to qualified immunity.

We appealed to the 9th Circuit to rehear the case before the entire 9th Circuit Court of Appeals; we wanted all seventeen judges to hear the arguments and make a decision. This appeal was granted and the case was argued before the entire panel.

Keep in mind; this entire process took *years*. In 2012, the case was scheduled on the docket and eventually it was argued before the entire Circuit Court of Appeals. Months pass before a written opinion was handed down. We lost nine to eight. Nine US appeals court judges ruled we were not entitled to qualified immunity and eight judges sided with us, agreeing that the lawsuit was baseless.

My attorney from the US Justice Department called me. He told me the Justice Department thought we had a very good chance if the United States Supreme Court would agree to hear the case, because the closely divided 9th Circuit Court and the extremely important issue of qualified immunity for Secret Service agents acting in their official capacity to protect the life of the President is in jeopardy.

If we lose this case on the qualified immunity issue, the future of the protective mission of the Secret Service is at stake—the Secret Service will have to take into account the "message" being voiced by citizens inside a secure area before the Secret Service can move them a safe distance from the President. Do you even know how ridiculous that sounds? It's as if a federal judge doesn't seem to think an assassin, lying in wait for the opportunity to kill the President, would not lie, "Oh, I'm just here to exercise my First Amendment right to disagree with the President. I'm not here to try an kill him."

"Yes," I said to my Justice Department attorney. "Let's file the appeal with the US Supreme Court."

The Supreme Court accepted the case and on March 26, 2014, I so wanted to pull out one of my old dark suits and sit in the back of the Supreme Court and listen to the arguments before those nine judges, but unfortunately, I was working for a living and missed the presentation.

I have spent a lot of time in federal courtrooms, and believe me, I have never been able to guess which way judges will rule just based on the questions they ask the lawyers. I have listened to the tape recording of the arguments presented to the Supreme Court. One minute I think Justice Kennedy is on my side, then it seems he's not. It sounds like Justice Kagan is leaning my way, and then she's not. Nerve-racking, completely nerve-racking.

On May 27, 2014, the US Supreme Court rendered its decision. The Justices voted nine to zero that this lawsuit was baseless and Agent Wood had a legitimate security rationale for moving the protesters, and thus were entitled to qualified immunity from lawsuits. I'd been retired for almost eight years and finally it was over.

I always knew this lawsuit would end in my (our) favor, but it sure took a long time. The lawsuit filed by the ACLU had a distinctive political point of view; they seemed to imply the Secret Service was acting as "protectors" of the President's political party. I've protected Democrats, Republicans, Communists, and dictators. The political party affiliation of the President is not a factor. Keep him alive and let the voters decide.

Epilogue

I was a Secret Service agent for twenty-one years, nine months, and five days. I was thirty-one years old when I took the oath of office in the LAFO on November 26, 1984. I was fifty-three when I retired on August 31, 2006, at the Seattle FO. Way too young to retire. I absolutely loved that job, and I so, so wish I could do it again.

After the Secret Service my retirement dream job was with the United States Olympic Committee as the director of security operations. I traveled with Team USA to international games locations and enjoyed the experience. Unfortunately, "security" seems to be a luxury with board members, and once the recession hit in 2008, my position was one of many cut when money got tight. But my old Las Vegas RA buddy B.J. came through and got me an interview with a new division in and old government agency. US Customs and Border Protection (CBP) had started an internal affairs division, and they needed experienced criminal investigators.

CBP gave me a four-year contract to investigate administrative and criminal cases against (suspected) corrupt border patrol agents and CBP officers. That was an interesting job, to say the least… there is nothing worse than a corrupt cop.

Those fours years flew by real fast and the next thing you know, I was unemployed again. Enter the Beaver and the Murphy Oil and Exploration Corporation. The Beaver called me and the next thing you know, I was working for the Beaver in deepest darkest Africa—Cameroon and Namibia. Providing security for expats living abroad, drilling for oil. I squeezed about thirteen months out of that gig, and then the price of oil plummeted, and once again, the board members decided "security" was a luxury.

Retired for good, I sat down at my computer and starting writing. This is what I wrote.

Acknowledgments

Al Joaquin, for giving me the thumbs up on that initial interview in Los Angeles; Skip Williams, Ralph Grayson and Stan Belitz for seeing promise in my panel interview. Earl Devaney for talking the SAIC into transferring me to Las Vegas. Chuck Brewster and Tom Spurlock, my RA's in Las Vegas. My cohorts in the desert— Mike Morgon, Rick Wadsworth, B.J. Flowers, Ron Weiss and of course the Beaver, Mike Fithen.

My Marine Corps buddies, Alan "Bronco" Bromka and Mark "Boots" Whitman and all the Bats of VMA(AW)242; it was a pleasure flying with you.

A special thanks to LtCol Robert L. Wills, USMC and Stephen Quinn.

CPSIA information can be obtained at www.ICGtesting.com
Printed in the USA
LVOW11s0309100316

478564LV00001B/31/P